S0-AHG-543

THE WIND HARP AND OTHER ANGEL TALES

The
Wind Harp
and
Other Angel Tales

Ethel Pochocki

ST. ANTHONY
MESSENGER

PRESS

CINCINNATI, OH

"The Angel in the Garden" previously appeared in *Cricket* (June/July, 1992). "The Wind Harp," "Isidore," "The Angels' Gifts" and "Sophia's Lullaby" previously appeared in *The Church World* (Brunswick, Maine).

Cover and inside illustrations by Mary Beth Owens
Cover and book design by Mary Alfieri
ISBN 0-86716-255-4

Copyright ©1995, Ethel Pochocki
All rights reserved.

Published by St. Anthony Messenger Press
Printed in the U.S.A.

Contents

To the angels,

who make life on earth

a joyous adventure

Foreword

These stories would have been written even if I had been holed up in some isolated Ecopod for the past decade, unable to read the best-seller lists and know that angels are a hot item, because I have loved angels all my life, way before they were *in*.

To me they are more than sentimental remnants of parochial school education or the pink cherubs of old holy cards. They are friends and companions along the way—at the moment invisible but no less real—who guide, inspire, warn, comfort and protect us from harm (and sometimes from ourselves). Without doubt they have a highly, or heavenly, developed sense of humor, for how else could they deal with us foolish, exasperating humans on a daily basis?

These stories are about testy, eccentric, lonely, proud, noble characters and the angels who touch their lives. "The Wind Harp," "Isidore and the Scarecrow," "Herschel and the Alien Corn" and "A Tree Full of Angels" are based on true incidents, but I have wrapped them in changes of time, place and characters so they are now strictly fiction.

Like the photographer in "A Tree Full of Angels," I pepper my walls with bits of inspiration.

One of my favorites is a Shaker saying, "Heaven and earth are threads from one loom." This book is for the angels, the spinners who weave and keep our wispy threads connected to Divinity.

The Wind Harp

A LONG, LONG TIME AGO, in a faraway
land of soft green hills and valleys, there lived
a farmer whose life was very lonely. You wouldn't
think he could be lonely, for he had a wife and
three daughters who never stopped fighting with
each other or scolding him, always yelling at the
tops of their voices. Sometimes his head ached with
the noise.

His was more a loneliness of the heart, a
sadness, as if he longed for someone or something
but he did not know what. He supposed he had
loved his wife once long ago, and he knew his
daughters had once been sweet, laughing babies,
but these women who gave him no peace with their
sharp tongues he did not know.

He took his solace from the small joys of his
daily life, working his scythe in the fields, watching
the silver salmon leap in the stream, listening to
the song of the lark at dawn and, best of all,
listening to the music of the wind. How he loved
the wind when it sang through the aspens and
sounded like the swishing of ocean waves! He
would add to the singing in the trees with chimes
he fashioned from scallop shells and scraps of thin
metal from the smithy, and when the wind
discovered them, he felt the joy of an artist who has
created beauty where it had not been before.

One wild, windy March day, as the chimes slapped against each other, he plowed the earth to plant peas and leeks, and the seed of an idea fell into his mind. The chimes were delicately lovely, but wouldn't the wind playing through the strings of a harp be even more glorious? Why couldn't he build a harp and place it on the crest of the hill that overlooked the sea? Here only cows grazed and ate the small, scabby fruit of the hawthorne and crabapple trees. It was a place that caught the wind from all directions. His heart quickened. Why not? Heavenly music to drown out the squawking from the henhouse!

The farmer had no idea how he would do this. He was a humble man, wise to the ways of earth, but unschooled in learning from books and the making of music. He had carved bowls from cherrywood burls, but this was of necessity, not passion. How would he go about making a harp large and strong enough to catch the wind?

He went into the Old Forest to confer with the Druid elders, who, when you found them in a good mood, were often willing to share their wisdom. The farmer presented his idea to them, and the learned circle nodded and agreed among themselves that such a harp would give glory to the spirits of the High Kings and to Aethe, priestess of the wind, and especially to their ancestors who once dwelled in the oaks the farmer would fell to make the harp.

And so they gave him their knowledge on how to build the harp, what materials to use and where to place it. They told him to call upon them when it was finished, and they would use their magic so it would stand forever.

The farmer chopped the sacred trees and dragged them out of the forest to an open field. He measured and sawed and chiseled and carved, and he rubbed the wood to a satin finish with sand from the shore. He went down to the trading ships whose dark-skinned captains spoke in a quick, strange tongue, and he begged and bartered apples and hazelnuts and wheels of cheese for brass and tin.

Through spring and summer and fall, he worked on the harp, following no book or master, relying only on the wisdom given by the elders and on his love for the wood to give form to his creation. On winter evenings, he sat before the fire, forging and twisting iron coils into the shape of fiddlehead ferns. These would hold the brass strings fast to the beams.

And all the while, his wife and daughters slapped their knees with laughter and whispered behind their hands and finally said right out loud what a foolish old man he was, making a harp only the wind could play! And then they went back to their gossiping and fighting.

Finally the farmer tightened the last of the eighty strings, and the harp was finished. The Druid priests and Aethe, in her green robes, came as they promised and set it into place, chanting the old prayers and offering it as an instrument for the gods to play. The farmer was achingly proud. Wherever he worked, he could look up and see it, standing like a noble sentry amidst the grazing cows, guardian of the farmer's land and even the village beyond.

The music it made was unlike anything the farmer had ever heard, and yet, it was as if he had always known it, a music from beyond earth. Each day the song was as different as the wind was different, and the sounds of treefrogs and crickets and church bells joined the wind as grace notes on its song.

From dawn to dawn, the music brought contentment to the farmer. In the evening, when the weather was warm, he often slept beneath the harp in its box, and he felt as if he were in the belly of a ship whose sails carried him aloft through moon-streaked skies. No longer was he sad or lonely, for the harp had satisfied his every need.

The farmer and the wind harp grew old together. When he died, it was not too long before the harp toppled and lay in the grass as if it too had died, for the Druids' magic worked only while the farmer lived. The oak frame and brass strings were soon taken over by woodbine and wild grapevines. Raspberry canes sprang up and stood guard over it. The daughters married and their mother went to live with the eldest, and the old farm was abandoned to creeping grasses and nesting mice. The years passed and the harp was forgotten by all but the wind.

Now at the same time, in another part of the green land, a young troubadour set off to make his fortune. He was not interested in money, but he did need *some* bit of fortune to buy a harp. His mind was so crammed full of stories he wanted to tell and sing, he feared they would all spill out and he would lose them. So he sang them aloud as he walked, to make them firm in memory, and wherever he stopped for food and lodging, he would tell his stories and sing his songs until the fire had turned to ash and even the children could not keep their eyes open.

Everyone said, "If only you had a harp...." Not, they assured him, that his voice alone was unpleasant, but a harp would embellish it, as a gold frame would a painting. He agreed, and began to save the coins they gave him. But if a beggar or poor mother looked needy, he emptied his pockets to the person. Yes, a sturdy little harp would be a joy, but it could wait. A hungry person could not.

A wise old woman said to him, "Go to Brigid, the holy woman of Kildare. She has the magic, she does. She will have a harp to suit you." So the young bard went to Kildare and knocked on the large carved door of the monastery, encouraged by the good smells and happy sounds of busyness within. The holy woman herself answered it. Everything about her was golden and blithe, from her hair to her laughter.

"Well, you're finally here, my young poet. I've been waiting for you. Come in, come in!" She embraced him and took off his raggedy cape. She welcomed him to the table and fed him cheese curds and oatcakes and ale until his cheeks turned rosy and his eyes sparkled and he could hardly contain the music bubbling up within him.

After the feasting, he sang for Brigid and her company of artists and scholars and holy men and women. He sang of kings and dragons and ladyloves and evil magicians, and everyone grew silent, touched by his sweet, pure voice.

When he finished, Brigid brought out a small lap harp, carved from holly and maple wood, crested with tiny jewels. She began to play and sing of things the troubadour had never heard. She sang about the Christian God, the God who reigned over trees and animals and human hearts, about the holy Mary and the saints in heaven.

The young poet felt strangely lighthearted and begged her to go on, to tell him more about this God who harmed no creature and loved even an insignificant singer. Brigid smiled, "Oh, poet, you have no idea how much you are loved and what songs you will give this earth! Now—take my harp. It's yours. Go your way and sing of God and his lovely world to all who will listen."

She kissed him gently on the forehead and placed the harp in his trembling hands. Then she went to the pantry and brought out a bottle of gooseberry wine and some currant scones, tied them up in her shawl and sent the troubadour on his way.

For a while, he was happier than he ever believed possible. Nothing was lacking in his life. He could imagine now what Brigid's heaven was like. But his happiness, and almost his life, came to an end when he was ambushed by bandits as he walked whistling through a wood.

They beat him and broke his hands and fingers

because he would not give up his harp without a struggle. They wrenched the harp from him, and even stole Brigid's shawl. The loss of the harp hurt him even more than his broken fingers.

He sat by the side of the road and begged not only for food but also to be fed, since he could not use his hands. He would sing to cover the pain, wondering if he would ever be able to use his fingers. Gradually, they healed and he moved them slowly, stiffly, but his fingers would not always do what his brain directed. He realized that he would never again be able to pluck the strings of a harp.

Through all this, he did not grow bitter. The sweetness of his voice was a clear reflection of his uncomplaining soul. Brigid said he was loved, and he would not doubt this. So he once again took to the road, his head filling with more songs, this time about God and the glories God had created. He spent his life walking, listening to the songs of lark and mourning dove, the woodcock's drumming and woodpecker's hammering, weaving them all into his songs.

He had accepted his life as it was and for the most part was not unhappy. Yet, now and then, the old yearning to play a harp pricked him like a bramble thorn in too deep to pull out.

One day when the poet, now old and lame and bent from facing the wind in his never-ending travels, took an unfamiliar dirt road that led to the sea. He could smell the salt and spring in the air on this first day of the fey month of March.

He knew there were yet fierce days ahead in

winter's death struggle. Nonetheless, he could smell spring. He longed to taste those first wild leeks which would give zest to his blood and mind, and to feel the harsh spring rain on his skin. His beard, white when clean, was now grey, matted and straggly. He was sure creatures were living in it, but he was so softhearted, he could not bear to evict them.

He stopped at the place where the farm once stood. The stones of the still-standing chimney were charred but unloosened. Windows were covered by honeysuckle vines. An old metal porridge pot lay rusted in a pile of rotting wood chips and curls from the farmer's knife.

The moonrise was full and silver bright. He thought he would sit by the chimney and imagine himself a fire. He gathered his ragged cape about him and closed his rheumy eyes. His nose, red and sore and scabbed over, began to run, and his allover weariness with life was great.

He heard a sound, like the gentle moaning of a young girl. Could it be the kelpies? The sea was nearby. He had not heard the kelpies since childhood.

The sound grew stronger, nearer. Now it was like the muffled sighing of the wind through a forest of aspens. The poet, not caring that he was lame, jumped up and ran painfully in the direction of the sound. Hand over hand he pulled himself up the slope to the meadow at top. His lungs ached from the icy air and for a moment he felt dizzy.

Then he was in the midst of the sound. It

surrounded him. His foot touched something long
and hard, not stone but wood. He reached down
and felt the old beams and the strings beneath the
carpet of woodbine. He ripped and tugged and
groaned until the vines were torn away and the
harp was revealed.

His mind could not comprehend what it saw.
What was this gigantic harp doing here? Why had
he been led to it, and what was he to do with it?

He was too weak to lift it. Yet he must, for he
felt a kinship with it. He knew that it was not a
harp for human hands, and that its song, like his,
was different from all others. "I know your music,"
he whispered to it. "I sing your songs. Our souls are
entwined, yours and mine."

He knelt back on his heels and bowed his head.
Tears blurred his eyes and made rivers down his
cheeks, almost turning to ice in the cold. He did
not care. But—how would he raise the harp?
"Lord," he cried out, "what shall I do? Help me!"

He covered his face with shaking hands, trying
to dry and warm his cheeks. Then, through his
fingers, tightly closed as they were, he could feel a
brilliant golden light. He peeked through the sides
of his cupped hands, and the light followed around
and behind him. He was immersed in it.

He heard laughter, as golden and spilled out as
the other time he heard it, and a voice called out,
"My young poet, here you are at last! It's been a
long journey, I know, poor dear. But now you're just
where you ought to be. Open your eyes. Don't be
afraid—look."

Slowly, fearfully, he opened his eyes. The brilliance was blinding and took some getting used to. He heard the great wrenching sound of the harp being torn from its tough, viny fetters. Three huge angels, in robes the colors of plums and limes and cherries, towering taller than the harp, were lifting and setting the harp upright and into place, just as the Druid elders had done so many years before, and the eager wind rushed into the strings as a lover into the arms of his beloved.

Brigid reached out and clasped the old man's hands into her own and kissed them. "Dear sweet singer, come, it's time to begin your new life," she said gently, and before he could wonder at her words, she pulled him from his body, as easily as if it were an old paper wrapper. Swiftly he soared with her, once again with the ruddy cheeks and clear eyes and supple hands of his youth.

"Because you have been true to your gift of song," said Brigid, "you have been chosen as Keeper of the Harp. You and the angels will guard it and make heavenly music here as long as earth exists, and all those who are lonely, wherever they are, will hear it and be consoled. They will know they are never alone."

And so the spirit of the searching poet finally found its home in the wind that played through the harp on the hilltop. It is said that the harp still stands on that hill that faces the sea, making music to which angels dance, waiting for another poet of pure heart to find it.

Sophia's Lullaby

SOPHIE KLOTSKI got off the elevator at the maternity floor, limped over to the nurses' station and signed in as the Volunteer Grandmother for Christmas Eve.

She wore, as usual, her long grey wool coat over the flowered housedress that zippered up the front, black laced shoes worn down at the heels and brown cotton stockings with lumpy veins showing through. Her sparse grey hair was pulled back tightly in a bun and her kindly face was a road map of age lines. She looked like many of the Volunteer Grandmothers, those noble souls who offered their time and laps to rock the newborns, so the nurses could attend to more pressing work.

The on-duty nurses were always pleased to see Sophie. They noticed she had an unusually calming effect on the babies fitfully struggling to adapt to their new world. She would rock them in her ample arms and sing them gentle songs in a strange language. One of the nurses who stopped to listen one night said she thought it was Polish. Another was sure it was Gaelic. Yet another swore it was Hungarian. Whatever it was, they were glad for it. "She's a real blessing," they said, and on a night such as this, they said it with added fervor.

Sophie moved down the corridor in her off-kilter gait—an arthritic hip, the nurses assumed—

nodding sweetly to those mothers up feeding their babies. When she reached the nursery, she hung up her coat, rubbed her gnarled hands together to warm them and waited.

A rosy glow began to gather about her, covering her from head to bunioned feet and Sophie Klotski disappeared within the cloud. From it emerged a motherly being of comforting beauty. She wore a billowing pink cotton gown and she smelled of apples and nutmeg and lilac talcum powder. Her thick, wavy chestnut hair was pulled back softly and held in place with two tortoise shell combs. The old woman had become who she truly was: Sophia, nursery angel in charge of welcoming the newborns.

Sophia went over to greet the ones awaiting her. Only seven tonight—such a small number! She remembered other hospitals, other Christmas Eves, over the centuries, when nurseries were crammed to overflowing and harried nurses grew weary with the bellowings of protest and hunger. Poor little ones, who could blame them? So far from home, dropped into a world of discomfort and needs and strange people calling them sons and daughters!

"There, there, no need to cry, here I am," she spoke soothingly as she walked from bassinet to bassinet, reading their names and smiling in recognition. One very red-faced baby was screaming so indignantly, she started the others crying as well. "Oh, Cecilia," she laughed, "you've discovered your lungs, I see. Always the loud mouth, the instigator, the one in charge—what a merry circus you'll make of life! All right, you'll be first, as you demand...."

Sophia picked up the chubby, dimpled child with masses of dark curls and held her firmly as she began to rock, their eyes meeting and, as it was back Home, understanding.

"Calm down, Cecilia," was the message Sophia sent. "There'll be time enough to use that voice. Listen and remember...." And she began to sing of Cecilia Emmanuela Aggramonte's life, in the way troubadours once sang of valorous deeds and noble lives.

Cecilia, she knew, was eager to use that voice that would one day electrify audiences in the opera houses of Paris and Milan. She had little patience with this infant body that could not yet contain her powerful voice. But in time, her glorious gift would come into its own and she would be the jewel in the family crown. Cecilia would be a happy, boisterous member of a happy, boisterous family—the ninth in a family of twelve children born to parents who owned a fruit and vegetable market—a family of chili pepper tempers, passionate convictions and deep loyalty. She would never marry, knowing that she was too tempestuous to be tethered to anyone, even in love. She would die in a plane crash at the age of 41, on her way to a Christmas Eve concert in Düsseldorf.

When Cecilia was sufficiently pacified, Sophia returned to her crib and picked up David Jonathan Solomon. Ah, David would have such an interesting life! His lullaby would be one of questing and paradox and mystery. In the beginning David, the only child of wealthy parents, would want for nothing. He would be bright, handsome, respectful—the kind of child most parents dream of having. He would graduate from Harvard, become a corporate lawyer, drive a red sports car, play polo and tennis, marry and divorce twice.

He should be happy, or at least content, but he was neither. One night he would take a walk in the woods on his estate and would have an encounter with his guardian angel, Herschel, who was sitting under a tree eating peanuts. They would talk through the night, about what only they and God would know. The next day David would give away his cashmere coats, his silk ties, his season tickets to the opera. He would say good-bye to his parents and leave his old life to live on an island off the coast of Scotland. Here he would spend his days as a hermit, growing vegetables, watching clouds, milking his goats, listening to the singing of seals and thanking God for all of it. He would at last be a happy man, to the bewilderment of his parents, who could never understand the madness that had possessed him.

Sophia tucked David into his receiving blanket and went next to Mary Ellen O'Connor, who was awake but not crying. Right from the beginning, she was a child who would not make a fuss. Mary Ellen was born to her parents late in their lives, an unexpected and not entirely welcome miracle. She would be a quiet child, unobtrusive as a mouse, a bookworm whose greatest joy would be reading fairytales in an old stuffed chair in the attic. She would be a dutiful child, giving neither pride nor distress to her parents, although they would be pleased when she became an algebra teacher.

Although she would have several suitors, none of whom she felt deeply about, she would not marry because she felt she must care for her aging parents. On the surface it would seem she lived a colorless existence. But unknown to anyone but God and her angels, Mary Ellen would have a secret life. In the evenings, in the privacy of her room, she would write mystery novels under the name of Francesca da Rimini, which, to her surprise, would be published and acclaimed and bring royalty checks of hefty size.

When her parents died, within months of each other, Mary Ellen would sell the house in which she had lived all her life, take her savings and go to live in a villa in Spain. At the age of 68, she would meet and marry a retired inspector from Scotland Yard. "My life," Mary Ellen would write in her autobiography, "is a fairytale writ by the hand of God."

Next to be Sophia's guest in the rocker was Bonnie Louise Bednarik, the first child of parents who owned a large dairy farm outside the city. Bonnie would live up to her name, a delightful child with laughing blue eyes, who loved animals as much as she did her parents. By the age of 10 she would declare her intention to be a veterinarian, but at the age of 12, she would die when she rushed into a burning barn to rescue her cat. Her heartbroken parents would establish a college scholarship in her name for needy students who wanted to work with animals and although they would have more children of their own, these young people, the Friends of Bonnie Louise, would be equally dear to them.

When it was James Joseph Johnson's turn to hear his song, Sophia told him first how lucky he was to be here at all. When his father knew James was on the way, he disappeared. James' mother, a soft-hearted young woman who could not kill a fly much less a baby, was turned out of her parents' home because she decided to have her child. She went to live with her grandmother, who was as happy then as she was today when James was born. His mother knew the hard road ahead of her, yet she knew this child would be a special gift to her.

James and his mother would be the best of friends when he was a child, but when he became a teenager, James would go off with his friends and hardly ever see her. He would begin to steal the things he wanted and finally, he would be caught with a leather jacket stuffed under his sweater and be sent to jail.

One night, when he was crying, thinking about his mother, his angel, Bertie, would sit on the edge of his cot and tell him of all the wonderful things he could do when he got back into the world and how he could use his gifts to change it, starting right now. And so James would become a model prisoner, working in the infirmary or library or wherever he was needed. When he was released the guards would shake his hand and wish him the best and call him James instead of Jimmy Jo.

James would become a practical nurse and he and his mother would move to Alabama, where he would work at a rural health clinic and where he would meet his future wife. "You have a lovely story, James," whispered Sophia, "remember it well during hard times."

Sophia glanced at the clock on the wall. Only twenty minutes until midnight and two more babies to be welcomed. She picked up LaVerne Jones, who was rooting around with her mouth and restless for her mother, but she would never see her mother, who had already put her up for adoption. "Don't fret, little one," said Sophia, "it will come out all right."

She knew that before the end of the week, LaVerne would be adopted by a childless couple who thought she was absolutely perfect and they would prove to be just as perfect parents. LaVerne would have a storybook life, a room of her own with a canopied bed, birthday parties and tap dancing lessons. She would sell Girl Scout cookies and win spelling bees and a college scholarship. And when she graduated, she would become a television journalist in Washington, D.C., and marry a Danish diplomat. She knew she had a privileged life, yet always below the surface happiness, like a subterranean stream, was the yearning ache to know her real parents and to know why they had not wanted her. She would try to find them, but she never would. Someday, Sophia assured her, when they all got back Home, they would find each other.

"And now for you, Raphael," she sighed deeply, as she cuddled the last child, just a bit more carefully than the others. She knew this one wanted to return Home as soon as possible. Raphael was born with withered, useless legs and he did not want to spend his time on earth crippled.

Sophia held him close as she rocked, quiet for the moment. Their eyes met. "I cannot stay," she read in his. "Never to be able to walk—I couldn't stand it. My heart is full of passion and rhythm— what shall I do with it? How can you ask me to spend my life in a wheelchair?"

"Yes, I know you'll never walk," said Sophia. "Or dance. Or ice-skate or ski or play with your children in the leaves. But is that all you think you are, a body without legs? You know better, Raphael Mendoza. You know God has sent you here for a purpose—do you think God would drop you and then cast you adrift?" She began her lullaby, singing softly of what his being here would mean to his parents.

"They love you so much, they prayed for you to come. They don't care that your body isn't perfect, they love you. If you give up without trying, a part of them will die too...."

Raphael blinked and yawned. Sophia continued, "In a few years, you will discover the violin and then you will go mad with delight over the beauty you can make. You will make others dance. Think of the children, the old people, the

lonely ones, who will be comforted by your music.
Raphael, it is your choice, but I ask you not to
refuse your life here. Even now your father is
lighting candles of thanks for your safe arrival and
your mother is counting the minutes until your
next feeding. Stay with them, Raphael!"

Raphael looked at Sophia with his wise, old,
newborn eyes. He tried to smile but hadn't quite
mastered the muscles yet. "All right. I've always
loved the violin. Are you sure I've got the gift? No
false promises?"

"Would an angel lie to you?" laughed Sophia,
rejoicing at Raphael's decision. She knew that once
his genius was discovered, he would be loved and
applauded for the rest of his life, which would be a
long one. And when he finally returned Home, he
would play his first concert standing up.

The minutes neared to midnight. Church bells
clanged and clattered in different parts of the city,
each echoing the other, calling the faithful to come
to the manger. The babies lay quiet, some sleeping,
some not, the hope and promise of Sophia's
lullabies settled in their souls and spilling out into
every pore and molecule and memory cell.

The nursery began to glow with a soft golden
light that was radiant but not blinding and within
the light there was a rising and falling, a busyness of
fluttering. Then, at the head of each of the seven
bassinets, there stood an enormous glowing being
with folded wings. They were so tall they had to
bend so their heads would not go through the
ceiling.

"Now, little ones," said Sophia, "let me introduce you to your lifetime friends. You will never be without them!" The glorious beings looked down upon the charges they would guard and guide until journey's end. Then Sophia kissed each child lightly, leaving them to dream one last, fading memory of Home.

In no time she was back into her housedress and wrinkled, aching body. She put on her coat, closed the nursery door and made her way back down to the nurses' station. The nurses wished her a joyous Christmas and insisted she take some gingerbread men home with her, which she politely did.

Then she took the elevator down, went out the hospital doors into the sharp frosty air and the happy muffled chatter of late churchgoers.

She could see clumps of angels already gathering in the sky and greeting each other, as they too hurried Home for the celebration. Sophia rushed to join them, hanging the gingerbread men on the nearest tree as a Christmas treat for the birds.

Isidore and the Scarecrow

LONG, LONG AGO in the country of
Spain, there lived a good, humble, God-loving
farmer. He was so good and humble and loved God
so much, he became a saint. It didn't happen all at
once, of course, nor was there any notice of it in his
lifetime. Only God knew the holiness of this man
who tilled so lovingly the spot of earth he had been
given. As with a painting, you had to stand a far
distance from his life to appreciate its beauty.

His name was Isidore—not Saint Isidore then,
just plain Isidore, husband of Maria, steward of a
landowner's farm outside Madrid. Maria was also
good and humble but had a quicker temper and less
patience than her husband. It is said that she, too,
became a saint, but we don't know why. Perhaps it
is because she spent her life living with one.

Isidore and Maria's home was a small white
stone cottage on the estate, near a grove of orange
and almond trees. Isidore said the fragrance of these
blossoming trees on a May morning was enough to
prove God exists. Every morning he would bound
out of bed (more slowly as age advanced in his
bones), run to the window and proclaim "Deo
Gracias!" to every lark and worm and swelling bud,
to the olive tree and barley field and shrubs of fig.
And out of the kitchen clatter, Maria would
answer, in a voice soft and preoccupied as a

mourning dove, "Deo Gracias."

Isidore spent his days in his fields, conversing with God as he walked behind the plow pulled by oxen, discussing the origin of boulders and the pungency of leeks, the benefits of ladybugs and the persistence of moles. He sang as he planted the garlic and tomatoes and ruffled basil and pruned the purple plums and rosy grapes. He sang songs to the sky, to the oxen, to the earthworms, to the bees eager for blossoms, and the wind carried them away to other fields and ears. He would think, at such times, if he died that night, he could not be happier.

His life was almost perfect, but not quite. "I don't mean to complain," he said to God, apologizing because he was. "I don't expect things to be perfect because this isn't Heaven, but—" There was a problem with the animals. He loved them all, from shrew to weasel. They were as much God's creations as all the green, growing things. And if he had been given dominion over them, it was a benevolent reign, doing them no harm.

The animals knew this and, having no fear, took advantage of his good nature. They did not even hide themselves during the day, but sat and chatted and watched as he plowed and hoed and sowed. Isidore was a good man and a friend, but they were not inclined to change their ways.

"It is our nature to eat peas," said the rabbits righteously.

"And corn," said the raccoons.

"And beans," said the woodchuck.

"And little red apples," said the deer.

"And little green onions," said the crows.

"And everything," said the mice.

Yes, admitted Isidore, all that was true. How could he ask the creatures to change? But was it fair to his master to let them eat their fill? What to do, what to do! He poured out his heart to God, as he mounded hills of dirt over the potato eyes, but God said nothing. That usually meant he would find the answer elsewhere. Very well, then, he must ask the angels.

The angels had been coming for some time now, whenever he called, two towering, shimmering creatures, magnificent in their gold and orange robes, their bronzed skin, their long, black curling hair that spread out like fans in the wind. Once they descended, they folded their wings neatly against their backs, so as not to call attention to themselves.

Isidore had been quite terrified when he first met these heavenly helpers—it had been during an invasion of Mexican bean beetles—for he had never seen an angel. He believed in them, of course, but assumed glimpses of them were only for the extremely holy or those about to die...had these come to carry him off, as an owl would a mouse? What would Maria think if he disappeared before the crops were in, without even a good-bye?

They reassured him and converted the beetles right on the spot, sending them back to Mexico where they rightfully belonged. After that, the angels came often, especially when Isidore's body

wearied, despite his willing spirit. They came once
with their own team of white oxen and plowed
alongside Isidore and his team, who were not at all
frightened of the strangers, until the fields were
harrowed fine and smooth and the color of cocoa.

At first Isidore didn't know how to address
them. "Your Magnificences," he stumbled, "Your
Graciousnesses, thank you so much. Are you—
special angels? In charge of emergencies?"

"No, we're guardian angels."

"Two of you?"

"Yes. It was decided you needed two. Please
don't ask us. We don't know God's mind any more
than you. We just follow orders."

"Oh, of course, I understand," said Isidore
quickly. He didn't want to offend them. But—he
had to ask—"Tell me, if you can—do you have
names? And, I always thought angels didn't have
bodies—you know, arms, muscles, hair, things like
that. I thought you were spirits."

The angels laughed and the hills echoed with
the marvelous peals. "We can take any shape we
choose. Sometimes it's better that we are small and
inconspicuous, but right now, good strong men are
needed to speed the plow, and so we are that! And
yes, we have names. I am Valerian," said one.

"And I am Bergamot," said the other.

Then, their work done, the angels and oxen
departed, the tremendous wings of the angels
casting the field in cool shade. "Call us anytime!"
cried Valerian as they disappeared.

And so Isidore did, on this day when he found

the baby pea tendrils nibbled to the ground and empty holes where the green onions had been planted. He heard the familiar great shivering of the air, as if wind had passed through a thousand aspens, and the angels were there.

They sat down beneath the pink-flowering almond and began eating oranges. "How can we help you, Isidore?" asked Valerian.

Isidore described his problem. The angels continued to eat and said nothing, deep in thought. They gathered the orange pips into silken pouches at their waists. To Isidore's unasked question they answered, "We will sow these where there is need of them."

They all talked together quietly. The angels suggested that he put a scarecrow in the vegetable garden, where most of the damage had been done. Isidore smiled and nodded, seeing the simple truth of what they said.

Yes, thought Isidore, a scarecrow, that would do it. It will frighten away the animals and still not hurt them. He thanked the angels and left them, hurrying into the woods with his axe. He returned with two pine saplings, tall and lithe, yet strong enough to bear their responsibility. He fashioned them into a cross, sweet-smelling with oozing resin, carried it to the garden and planted it securely in the midst of the leeks and cabbages.

Now, how to clothe it to fool the animals into thinking it an unfamiliar, threatening stranger? The angels had suggested a dress. Surely his wife had a dress to spare.

Of course! Maria would be glad to give one for such a worthy cause.

He went to the cottage to ask her, but Maria was in the village selling eggs. He opened her closet, picked out a bright red dress with lace collar, ribboned sleeves and small black shining buttons down the front. This would do nicely, something to catch the animals' eyes when they came out of the woods. Then he lifted Maria's straw hat from its peg, the Sunday one with cherries pinned to the band of red and white ribbons.

He pulled the dress over the pine limbs, and the skirt blew into bellows in the soft wind. Then he nailed the hat onto the top of the cross. At the end of the tree-arms, he hung chimes of glass. All in all, he had created a pleasant but firm housewifely scarecrow, watching over her garden and suffering no intruders. He could hardly wait to show Maria.

Without warning, two rude crows swooped down and brazenly began pulling at the ribbons and buttons and cherries, screeching in raucous triumph. Maria, who had just arrived home, heard the racket and came running.

When she saw her pride and joy, her lovely Sunday dress which had been a gift from the mistress, being torn at and ripped and soiled by the crows, and Isidore flapping around the scarecrow hag like a bewildered bird and the rusty nail hammered into the crown of her hat, she began shrieking and sobbing and holding her head.

This was not what Isidore had expected. But Maria, for all her goodness, was quite human, and she did not like anyone, even her husband, disturbing her clothes. Finally, when she regained her reason, she took the dress and hat from the cross, still sniffling to herself, and walked home in silence.

Isidore apologized, blaming just a little of his actions on the angels. Maria forgave him, with some effort, and fixed up the dress with new ribbons and white pearl buttons. She darned a small rosebud over the hole in the hat. The clothes were serviceable and she wore them, but with a sense of duty now and not excitement. She wished the angels would stick to more holy things in the future.

His scarecrow stripped, Isidore again called upon the angels. They came, in that cloud of golden haze that announced them, and heard his sorry tale.

"I don't understand why she was angry," said Valerian. "A dress is a dress, isn't it?"

"Perhaps," said Bergamot, rubbing his noble chin, "one dress could be more important than another?"

"I don't understand women," sighed Isidore. All three nodded and pondered the mystery of women. Then Valerian said they should move on to the larger problem of the animals.

"Perhaps," he said, "we are going about this in the wrong way, working through fear, not love— perhaps a different kind of scarecrow, one that doesn't scare, one that attracts—"

"Ah, yes," said Bergamot, "I can see where

you're going with this."

They explained their idea to the puzzled Isidore. Obediently, he went to the potting shed, which still smelled of last year's mint and lavender hanging in dried bunches from the ceiling. He put some seeds into his pocket, picked up the shovel and went into the woods. He dug up two small vines just coming into leaf.

He went to the garden and at the bottom of the naked cross, he planted the two roots of bittersweet and honeysuckle and several seeds of morning glory and trumpet vine.

Then, around the garden he fashioned a fence of pine boughs, weaving their soft green needles together tight as locked-arms. At the base of the fence, all the way around, he planted peas and covered them, and on top of that, lettuce and parsley and chard.

"Now," he smiled, "my dear rabbits and skunks and little ones, you will have all you can eat, and the pea vines will make a sturdy wall to protect my master's peas. Everyone will be satisfied."

Before long, the bare cross was clothed in a mingling of different-shaped leaves, each entwining the other, and soon after that came the flowers, and then the berries. In the morning, before the others awoke, the purple and blue trumpets of the morning glories piped their greetings, and the honeysuckle lured the bees with their sweetness. The scarlet trumpet flowers were filled with nectar-hungry hummingbirds. The bittersweet circled in and out, knowing that when the blooms were gone, its orange berries would still delight.

Isidore's scarecrow scared no living thing. It was simply an angelic vision, you might say, that nourished birds and bees and all who could never resist even a crumb of beauty.

Nor were his crops ever again bothered by the animals. It may have been that they were so touched by Isidore's kindness that they responded in like manner, as the God within them would have it. True, an occasional rambunctious rabbit might eat his way through the fence and feast, but for the most part, the master received his full measure with enough left over for Maria to can and pickle for the winter.

For the rest of his life, Isidore and the angels enjoyed each other's company, even when there was no emergency to bring them together. Once, after a long day of cutting hay, he invited them home, and they accepted. Maria was not overjoyed to have uninvited guests, even celestial ones, and when she saw their tremendous wings, she became quite unraveled. Even neatly folded, they barely fit in a room not built for angels.

But she remembered her manners and made them comfortable. She considered bringing them a basin of water to wash their feet, but she did not know if angels had feet, and she was too embarrassed to ask, so she did not.

When they left, each carrying a gift of melon, Maria tried to catch a look as they flew off, but the golden haze was too thick to pierce. She was left to

puzzle over the existence of angelic feet, much as
the angels had over the mystery of women and their
dresses.

Lefty and Lazarus

THERE WAS ONCE a cat nobody loved, not even his mother. He was long and lean and black, and his name was Lefty.

He was a street cat, tough and smart, abandoned by his mother when he was just a babe. He lived by the trash can where she dropped him, learning quickly where to find food and hide and sleep. He walked all over town, wandering into bars, where he drank beer from a saucer, and the health food shop, where he acquired a taste for herbed cheese and tofu. He sometimes made it into the laundromat, lured by the warmth, but he was usually chased out by people intent on cleanliness.

One day, a young woman riding a bicycle knocked him down. She picked him up and felt his little heart beating frantically. "You poor little thing, I'm so sorry!" she stroked him and held him close. "And you're so thin. I bet you live on garbage and leftovers. How would you like to come home with me, little leftover?"

Without waiting for an answer, she tucked the bewildered cat into her basket and wheeled off.

And so, Lefty came into a real home, but he was still a creature of wild habits. Curtains, shades, rocking chairs—all bore marks of his attack. He upset and broke flower-painted bowls of candy. He dug up geraniums from their pots and flung their

dying bodies around the room. He stole food from
the table, licked the butter, dipped his paw into the
cream and picked the cheese out of his mistress'
salad. At night he slept on her pillow and snored
and wheezed, but she never complained; she just
moved over and pulled the blanket about her ears.
Lefty, for so she named him, had taken over house
and mistress and could do no wrong.

On the good side (his mistress made lists of his
good and bad points, trying in vain to make them
balance), he did catch mice. One morning he had
demolished four mice before 11 A.M. He felt this
gave him the right to tear apart the mail that had
come through the slot on the porch. As he chewed
thoughtfully on a magazine, he saw a small deer
mouse staring at him rather boldly. The mouse sat
as if waiting to be noticed by the cat.

Lefty, giving his hunter's cackle, leapt and
caught the mouse and tossed him into the air.
When he landed, the cat put his paw on him firmly,
but still allowed him to wriggle. He would tease and
taunt him for a while before making a mid-morning
snack out of him.

"Lefty," said the little brown mouse quietly, "let
me go. I'm your guardian angel."

The merciless hunter had heard many mouse-
pleas in his time, most of which he ignored, but
none so ridiculous as this. Why did the mice fight
simple logic, he sighed—a cat catches a mouse and
he eats him. It was the rule. If mice were as
intelligent as cats, they would develop quick escape
strategies. They should learn to elude danger, not

plead for mercy when caught. It took away their dignity.

Now this mouse claimed to be his guardian angel! He opened his mouth to laugh, and the mouse, now held in it, slid between his teeth. He bounded up to the ceiling where he hung by his feet.

Lefty gaped, his eyes widening. "Will you listen to me?" called the mouse, swaying gently with his paws clasped behind his head.

This is no ordinary mouse, thought Lefty. It might be best to humor him. Once he was down and within grasp, that would be the end of him. For now, Lefty would feign interest.

"You intrigue me, mouse. Come down here and tell me how you do that trick. Do you think I might learn?" he asked silkily.

"Only if you cast out the evil thoughts in your heart. I'm not about to be your next meal."

This is definitely one strange mouse, thought the cat. The mouse was now flying about the room, well out of Lefty's reach, landing on lampshades, balancing on curtain rods. Lefty tried to appear unimpressed.

"You don't really expect me to believe you're my guardian angel, do you? A guardian angel mouse? Really!"

"Why not?"

"Cats don't have angels for one thing, if there even are angels. Only humans have them. They get all the good stuff. We're supposed to be the lower order, you know," he sniffed.

"Everyone has a guardian angel, every living thing."

"Oh, I'm sure. Must be pretty crowded up there with all those angels flying around. Had any mid-air collisions lately? Be logical. If everyone had an angel, every animal and hollyhock and sardine, there'd be no place to turn around, no room to breathe." Lefty thought, "I can't believe this. I am arguing with a mouse."

The mouse, sitting in the shamrock plant on top of the piano, smiled and preened his whiskers. "Lefty, you are thinking with your small feline mind. Believe me, there is room. There is magnificence. There is order. Everything fits. And we angels are real, with real jobs. We do praising, combat-fighting, soul-saving, message-delivering. Mostly, though, we guard. We get our assignment and stay with it from birth to death and then start all over again. If I choose to be seen, I can be anything I want—a child, a man in a brown suit, a bag lady, a mouse.... Once I was a ginger tomcat. I let my human see me, a lonely old grouch of a lady, so she could have someone to love."

"And now you're mine," yawned Lefty. "I'll believe that when—"

"When mice fly?" laughed the mouse.

"I'll admit that's a good trick. Listen, even if you are an angel, just think how it would look—me, the street cat, going around with a mouse. A black cat and a brown mouse, strolling along as though we're the best of friends. My mother, God rest her, would turn over in her grave, if she had a grave."

The mouse shrugged. "That's the way it is. We get our assignments, assume the body and go to work. It could be worse. I could be a Doberman Pinscher—like this—" And the mouse became a huge black dog with elfin ears, his lips grimacing like silent lightning. Lefty's body froze and his tail grew six inches around.

"Or a gorilla—"

Lefty felt himself lifted up into the palm of a hairy creature who stroked him and kissed him with wet lips and then tossed him from palm to palm.

"Stop!" cried the cat. "I'm getting sick! A mouse is fine. A mouse is wonderful. I believe you!"

"A mouse," said the angel, now returned to mouse size, "will make you humble. You could use some humility. To walk with me, be seen with me as an equal, that will take some doing. But you're a cat who can adapt, you can do it."

"Why can't you be invisible? Guard me if you will, but don't show yourself to anyone else."

"Not this time, Lefty. Lefty—wherever did you get that name?"

Lefty bristled. He knew his name was not elegant, but it was his mistress' doing, not his. "Don't angels have manners? You're so high and mighty, but you still make fun of someone's name. What's yours, anyway, if mouse angels have names?"

"Lazarus."

Lefty snorted. "That's a real pip."

"I agree. But it's my own fault. The day we were given names—they were up to the La's in the alphabet—I was having too good a time flying over Omaha and by the time I got back, all the good ones were gone. I really wanted Lancelot, but of course that went quickly. So did Laddie, Lackadaisy, Latterday, Lafcadio, Lafayette, Lavender, Lastminute—all gone but Lazarus. Quite appropriate," chuckled the mouse, "seeing as I'm almost risen from the dead."

Lefty made no comment to that. "Now what am I supposed to do—be good? Pray every morning and evening? Don't steal cheese or chase birds? Dream on, mouse!"

"Just be yourself. I like a challenge. But don't expect me to keep you out of trouble if you don't listen to me. Still, if you ever really need me, I'll be there in a flash."

And so, gradually, the cat grew accustomed to the mouse accompanying him on his daily adventures. Lazarus found himself called upon for immediate rescue more often than either imagined, for Lefty attracted trouble like lint. In besting traffic, traps, mean humans and the cat's own inclination to mischief, Lazarus became to him as Saint Michael with the flaming sword, protector of the weak and helpless.

He taught the cat how to weave warily through traffic and to look both ways before crossing and not depend on his ears alone. Once, when Lefty forgot the angel's warnings and dashed into the street and caused two trucks to collide, Lazarus turned himself into a parade of soldiers to divert the angry drivers. They marched past with the flag held high, and cars screeched and bumped and stopped, and the drivers got out and held their hands over their hearts in respect. And the parade disappeared around the corner with Lefty in its wake.

Each day brought its own hairbreadth escape. When Lefty, chasing a chipmunk, found himself stranded at the top of a very tall tree, Lazarus turned into a giraffe and let him slide down his neck. When Lefty was about to be beaten by a housewife with a broom for stripping her catnip plants, Lazarus became a unicorn with lavender eyes and a collar of rubies. He stood, proud and beautiful, in the midst of her cabbages. The housewife dropped her broom, walked into her house and quietly closed the door.

Once, when the cat was cornered by a gang of nasty boys, intent on catching him for their own dark purposes, a swishing shower of sparks lit up the sky and they stopped throwing cans at him and stared. A giant mouse with a red beret and satin cape was flying through the sky directly towards them. When he landed the earth shook and he picked up the boys and hurled them through the air until each landed in his own backyard. They never spoke of this to anyone, and from that day they avoided all cats and mice.

Lefty had grown so used to sharing his life with the angel, he thought it would go on this way forever. But it did not. One evening, as the two sat enjoying the first concert of the spring peepers in the swamp, breathing deeply the smell of sweet fern and new earth, a shadow crossed the moon and a

snow owl plummeted to earth. He snatched the
mouse up in his talons. Lefty hissed and howled his
crackly cry, but it was no use. They were gone.

His heart hung heavy with sadness, and he
began the walk home. How strange not to have the
mouse beside him. They had grown so close in the
time they had together. Now who would protect
him? He stopped and looked up at the moon,
hoping he might see his angel flying over it. And
then he thought. If his angel was his guardian for
life, and he, Lefty, was not yet dead, then—? His
grief began to lift like a morning fog. Then Lazarus
would surely rise and come again!

He awaited the angel's second coming and new
guise. It could be any creature who passed through
his world. He would be alert to all possibilities. So
it was the next morning, when he noticed a large
crow loitering in the garden, that he ran speedily,
joyously, to the bird and rubbed against him.

"Do you have a problem?" asked the bird icily.

"Come on, Lazarus, you can't fool me. I'd know
you anywhere!" purred the cat.

The crow jabbed him sharply in the head with
his beak and flew off. Lefty spent the rest of the day
under the yew bush, regaining his senses. His angel,
he decided, would not lower himself to be a crow.

In the evening, as he meandered through
sleeping daffodils, a bat swooped out of the barn
cupola and slid down a wind gust into the garden.
"Lazarus!" cackled Lefty softly. "Of course, you'd be
a bat, not a crow!" He tried to rub noses with the
startled bat, who flew quickly back to the cupola.

"All right, no crow, no bat. But whatever you will be, Lazarus, I am ready for you."

The next day he went to the woods, hoping to find the angel in squirrel or chipmunk or rabbit, but the animals ran from him, except a fox who looked him straight in the eye and said nothing.

Disappointed, he sat in the sunporch window awaiting his mistress. A newcomer to the neighborhood came by with a sheepdog on a leash and Lefty had a moment of panic. But they just looked at him and passed by. His mistress finally came up the walk, and she carried a small box with a handle. She spoke to it softly. "There, there, old fellow, don't you fret. I'll take care of you. You won't have to worry about anything any more. Wait till you meet Lefty...."

Lefty sat very still, his tail switching in little jerks. His mistress opened the box and an old ginger tomcat pawed his way out and stretched.

"That has got to be the ugliest cat I've ever seen," thought Lefty, not wanting to stare but fascinated by the sight. The tomcat looked to be a veteran of many wars, few of them victorious. His ears were nicked and bent and one eye closed permanently. He limped on one back leg and his two front paws were flattened like pancakes from the time he had been caught in a trap. He smiled broadly at Lefty and began to drool.

Lefty groaned. How could you, Lazarus!

The tomcat limped over and sniffed Lefty's fur.

"Oh, isn't that sweet, Lefty, he wants to be friends!" sighed his mistress. "I just knew you two would get along. Isn't he a sweet old fellow? He just came in today at the animal shelter."

Lefty looked Lazarus in the eye, the open eye, and winked. "Couldn't you at least manage a decent coat? Don't you ever think about my reputation?"

Lazarus rolled on his back in ecstasy. A streak of tar and several thistle burrs marred the soft orange belly.

"Humility, Lefty. We have to work on your humility."

"What shall we call him?" wondered his mistress. "Something that would fit a survivor."

"What's wrong with Lazarus?" thought Lefty, hoping she would read his mind.

"Something like...Spike...Old Yeller...Ginger Tom...Hardhat...Mulligatawny...Mr. Oddfellow...Born Again...Robbie Crusoe...." She walked away muttering and trying on names as if they were hats.

The cat and the angel, together once more, rubbed noses lovingly.

The Poppy Angel

IN A GARDEN of beautiful flowers, there grew a poppy who thought herself the most beautiful of all and, in truth, she was. She was tall and strong, towering above her sister poppies and foxglove and sweet william and larkspur. Her purply scarlet satin petals were double ruffled, like petticoats under a dancing gown. She was the only one of her kind. Where she had come from or what mischievous wind had brought her was a mystery.

The poppy stood out, catching every eye, and she reveled in being the center of attention. She had no false modesty about this. "I am beautiful beyond compare," she preened proudly as the wind ruffled her petticoats.

"But I am stronger than you," teased the wind, "and I can make you dance, whether you like it or not!"

The poppy only laughed because she knew better. "Oh blow away, you old thing," she teased the wind right back. "I shall dance but only if I choose.

I will not bow,
I will not bend,
My beauty is such
It has no end!"

The other flowers shook their heads at her
boldness, but they were not jealous, for despite her
high opinion of herself, the poppy had a kind heart.
If she acted like an elegant queen, she was a merry
and generous queen as well. She welcomed all to
her court—birds, bees, butterflies, hummingbirds,
an occasional inchworm who crawled into her
petals to take a nap. As long as they paid her proper
respect, she enjoyed them all.

Unfortunately, the queen's reign was not long.
The scarlet petals turned dull, curled up and
dropped off. The poppy looked quite different now.
She was still tall and strong and green, but with the
petals gone, her face could be seen. It was round
and full as a doll's chowder bowl and a crown of
thirteen stars sat upon her head. Now she looked
like a jolly, middle-aged queen who no longer
thought of being fashionable.

The wind howled around her gleefully and tried
to make her bend and bow, but she would not. "Just
wait a few weeks when you're brittle and brown," he
laughed, "you won't be so proud then, my fine lady!
You'll be just like the rest of them."

That time did come, when leaves began to fall
and nothing remained flowering in the garden but
wild clover and Michaelmas daisies. The smaller
poppies huddled together, shivering in their
nakedness and whispering quietly among
themselves, their crowns head to head. Soon, they
gossiped, they would be picked to be used in dried
bouquets, along with the milkweed pods and
cattails from the swamp.

The poppy listened and shrugged. She knew
that would never happen to her. She would not
bend and she would not bow and she would never
be stuck in a bunch of anything. She was not, after
all, just another poppy.

Before any of the flowers was picked, a young
woman came into the garden from out of the woods.
She had been gathering grapevine for wreaths and
hops for sleep pillows which she would sell at
autumn fairs. She was tall and strong and wore a
long red dress and a straw hat with a wide brim. The
poppy watched her with approval. She was almost
as lovely as the poppy had been in her youth.

The young woman stopped by the garden and
gazed at the proud poppy stalk. "Well, look at you,"
the young woman smiled, "you're extraordinary.
I've never seen such a round face.... Someone
should do something with you."

As the woman stood there, the sun, the golden
sun of September afternoons, came through the
trees in thin fingers of gold and bathed the poppy in
a shimmery light and she seemed to have a halo
over her crown.

"An angel!" exclaimed the young woman.
"You're an angel!" She knew right then and there
what she would do with the poppy. She snapped the
dry stem, shook the seeds from the round pod into
her hankie, tied the ends together tightly, stuck it
into the pocket of her dress and carried her
treasures home.

Late into the night she worked, trying to make
the poppy into the vision of the angel she had seen

in the garden, until it finally came right. By dawn, her eyes were heavy, her fingers sore, her body stiff, but her spirit was giddy as a bubble, for her angel was finished.

The poppy-stalk body had been swathed in layers of cotton to fill her out and over this hung a gown of gauzy cheesecloth which the young woman had dipped into beet juice to make it a deep purply crimson. A shawl of the same color was tossed lightly around the angel's shoulders. Her arms, which reached out in loving welcome, were made of wire and covered tightly with white gauze and bound with thread, as if she were wearing long white gloves.

Golden wild grasses drooped from her shoulders in the shape of wings and driplets of hardened wax, like the winter dew, clung to the lacy ends. Her face and crown were framed in a halo of milkweed down. As the morning sun shone through the window onto the angel, the young woman thought she had never seen a more heavenly sight.

She tied a small golden string where the two wings met and hung the angel from a nail above the window. As she drank her morning coffee, she sat and admired it and wondered what she would do with it.

At first, she thought she would keep it; she could not bear to part with it. But then, like a mother with a newborn baby, she yearned to show off her creation and hear exclamations of delight over her offspring. She decided she would bring the angel to the craft fair—just to show, not to sell.

And so she did. As she knew they would, the people flocked around her stall admiring and wanting to buy the angel, but she would not sell and the people moved away. One gentleman did not go. He stood quietly before the angel, never taking his eyes off it, his thumb under his chin, his forefinger tapping his lips.

Finally he spoke. "I know you do not want to sell your angel. If I had made such a magnificent thing, I would not either. But—would you consider sharing it with others who need her beauty—children and old folks and sad folks and people who don't have gardens? Someplace where she would live forever and be treated with great care?"

The young woman was quite puzzled by all he said. He explained that he was the head of a museum in a large city, where every year a gigantic Christmas tree was mounted in the hallway, right in the center of spiraling marble staircases and crystal chandeliers. On this tree were hung priceless ornaments from every corner of the world—glass swans from Germany, wooden clowns from Sweden, homespun cornhusk dolls from Kentucky, straw doves from Mexico, snow globes that played music—

"And at the top," he said, "under the star, would hang the poppy angel. Not just this year, but every year. She would live forever. Or reasonably close to that."

"Say yes!" yearned the poppy angel. She very much liked the idea of again being the center of attention and holding court in a new garden. She

was of course grateful to the young woman for
having transformed her, but she certainly didn't
want to live in that dreary cottage forever.

The young woman hesitated, for she was torn
between keeping and sharing, but she finally
agreed, for she was not a selfish person at heart. The
gentleman paid her handsomely and also bought a
grapevine wreath for his wife and a sleep pillow for
his train ride home. The young woman wrapped the
poppy angel in layers of tissue paper, packed her
into a sturdy box for carrying and bade her farewell.

She was sad to say good-bye to the angel, but
under the sadness, she felt a smile. She reached in
her dress pocket for the hankie with the seeds she
had shaken from the poppy's pod. She would plant
them this very day for spring blooming.

As the gentleman had foretold, the poppy angel
drew all eyes to where she hung on the magnificent
Christmas tree. The poppy, no more humble as an
angel than a flower, was not surprised. She had
survived wind and frost and old age. She had not
bowed or bent or been picked to gather dust in
dried bouquets with teasel and Japanese lanterns
and other old relics. Now she reigned again.

"Of all the beautiful ornaments on this tree,"
she preened in absolute contentment, "I am the
most beautiful of them all."

Her pride was an honest, not boastful, one, for
the beauty she had been given had been returned
wholeheartedly to praise the Christ child in the
crèche. Because of him, she had reason to live
again.

In truth, the poppy with her gift of self, the young woman with her gift of seeing and her skill in making it real, and the gentleman with his gift of wisdom, all gave praise in a manner worthy of such pride.

Herschel and the Alien Corn

HERSCHEL SAT ON THE SILL of
heaven, dangling his strong, muscled legs in space,
as if he were a human child splashing about in a
stream, enjoying the last moments of bliss before he
left for the new assignment.

He stretched his magnificent angelic body,
powerful as a battalion of soldiers (indeed, he once
was a battalion during the Genghis Khan
incidents), his crisp, curly hair and black skin
shining like satin in the celestial sun. He opened
and spread his coffee-colored wings, which
matched his gown, to full expression, savoring the
pleasure. Soon enough he would be confined to the
limits of a raven's wingspan.

Herschel knew the mission would be a
challenge. Ruth, the human, would be a tough old
bird to convince. He smiled at his choice of words,
then chuckled out loud in anticipation of what lay
ahead. He took on all missions with zest, but, he
had to admit, some were more fun than others.
(The IRA stint had not been fun.) Just how much
fun this one would be depended on Ruth—she had
to make the choice.

Ruth had been under consideration for
heavenly intervention for quite a while, and the
judgment had come down that *now* was the time.
Even before she and her parents and baby brother

had emigrated to the United States from Puerto Rico, she had been a source of observation and amusement for the angels as a specimen of human as intricately fashioned as a fine Swiss clock.

From birth, Ruth had been strong-willed and feisty, demanding that her needs be met promptly. As she grew older, she added a talent for argument and a certainty that she was always right. Her compassionate heart, known only to God and the angels, was well-fortressed within her don't-tread-on-me actions.

She had lived with her parents in the apartment above their store, taking care of their needs and tending to her baby brother as if he were her own, until her parents died and her brother returned to Puerto Rico. Ruth had not married. Her mother had warned that no man would want anyone with such a mouth on her, so rather than test the theory, Ruth chose, she said with belligerent pride, not to be shackled to any man.

Now old, her joints and limbs as stiff as her pride, she kept to the apartment, asking nothing from government or neighbor, venturing out for groceries or church, sometimes to wakes and funerals for the old-timers who had not left the neighborhood. When they first came here, the place was a heady mixture of skin colors and strange languages and clothing and pushcarts loaded with bagels and dried mushrooms and smoked herring, and, over all, the wonderful smells of food cooking. There were children playing stickball in the street and mothers calling them home and hanging wash on pulley lines between buildings.

Everyone knew everyone else and everyone else's business. Now it was so different. There were many more languages and styles of dress and outrageous things like nose rings and hair the color of a Sunkist orange. The pushcarts were gone, replaced at every corner with hot dog and pretzel and coffee stands.

What Ruth missed most of all was the kindness and trust of caring neighbors. Now everyone locked their doors and ignored each other, wouldn't even say hello, just looked away. The children, who were once a source of comfort and help, running errands, shoveling snow, looking in on the old folks, now were rude, annoying and just another cause of fear.

She particularly did not like the black boys who hung around corners, laughing loud, slapping each other, blaring those obnoxious big radios. Ruth didn't think she was prejudiced—Lord knows, they had known enough of that—but these kids had trouble stamped all over them.

Even though she felt menaced by them, she wouldn't let them keep her from her appointed rounds. She warned anyone who would listen that kids who had bad things on their minds had better not tangle with her. One rainy afternoon, one of the boys tried to yank her purse out of her hand. She whirled around to face him, all her fear now turned to anger, and whacked him and the rest of them, each in turn, with her umbrella, dancing around and pointing the tip at them as if she were fencing.

Then she whipped out a can of red pepper from her pocket and shook it in the air, hoping it would find its mark. She blew on the police whistle that hung around her neck, with a medal of Saint Dymphna, patroness of nervous disorders, attached to it. (It had come in the mail and she couldn't figure where else to put it.)

The old lady dancing around on her chicken legs, dueling with her umbrella, was so funny that the boys not already incapacitated by umbrella wounds and pepper fell to the ground laughing. Ruth gave them each one more jab and continued on her way. The boys nicknamed her "The Samurai" and kept their distance from her after that.

Ruth's life within her apartment was quite different from her outside adventures. Here she allowed tenderness, gentleness, remembrance of the past. Mementos of her childhood, Christmas dolls and worn storybooks, photos of her parents and baby brother (now married with a family of six), displayed in frames, sat on any unoccupied flat surface. Birthday cards and Christmas cards of the baby Jesus under a palm tree from her brother were pinned to the wall. This is my life, all of it, she thought sadly. All the good things were in the past, gone. Every day was now the same, survival until the next and then do it again. She supposed this is how it would be until she died and joined her parents.

But something in her rebelled at the prospect, for she was not by nature a resigned person. She

still felt a flicker, a yearning for something.
Adventure, challenge, something to shake up the
unremitting placidity of her days. This was her
restless mood one spring evening as she sat on the
fire escape, watching the kids in the street jumping
rope—one thing left over from the old days—and
breathing in the smells of truck exhaust and fish
frying in overheated grease.

She found some comfort in the unchanging
pattern of the stars. She wondered if Queen
Elizabeth, glancing out her palace window, saw the
same stars, and what she thought about them. She
wondered if her brother in Puerto Rico might look
up and see this very sight. No, of course not, it
would be more beautiful there.

Tonight, after she had taken out her memories,
shuffled and cut them and lay them out to be turned
over slowly one by one, she had treated herself to a
bowl of popcorn made in a frying pan on the stove.
Usually she burned it and had to live with the smell
for days, but tonight it had turned out just right.
Another small comfort.

She was about to get up and sprinkle some
parmesan cheese on the popcorn, when a large bird
dropped out of the sky and sat down beside her.
Ruth looked at it warily and sat very still. He was
the largest crow she had ever seen. He might be an
omen of death. Or he might peck her eyes out. The
crow was looking at her very intently, with an
unblinking, steadfast gaze. It had a small orange
velvet pouch around its neck.

"Good evening, Ruth," the crow said in a voice

as deep and dramatic as an opera baritone. Ruth stopped eating and looked at her bowl. The bird was talking. In a human voice. She knew the mind could go when you got old, but she wasn't that old. She knew what day it was and her birthday and could add up her grocery bill faster than the cash register.

"Good evening, Ruth," the raven repeated. "It's rather warm for April, isn't it? I hope you don't mind my joining you, but I've come to bring you a gift."

"How can you be talking to me?" asked Ruth without taking her eyes from the bowl. "You're a crow."

"Well, no, I'm a raven."

"Crow, raven, what's the difference. You're a bird and you're talking to me."

"The difference is that a raven is another species of crow, somewhat more upscale, higher in intelligence. But that's neither here nor there, since I'm not really a bird. I'm an angel, and my name is Herschel."

Ruth wondered if she might be having a slight stroke, or perhaps a hallucination. What had she been eating lately? Or, she might be crazy. Either way, she decided to keep the conversation going to see just how ridiculous it could get.

"Right, you're an angel. So if you're an angel, how come you're dressed up like a yuppie crow?"

"We dress to suit the occasion. This seemed most appropriate, inconspicuous. Birds come and go, don't attract attention. The thing is, do you believe I'm an angel?"

Ruth laughed. "Why not? If I can believe a bird is talking to me, I can believe you're an angel. The sky's the limit. Crazy is crazy, what difference does a little more make? So, tell me, what do you really look like, you know—Up There?"

"You'd be surprised," Herschel laughed so heartily, so loud, Ruth feared everyone would hear and traffic would stop, but the people kept on walking and the children played and fought and no one looked up.

"So where's the gift?" said Ruth, eying the pouch.

"Take the pouch off my neck and open it."

She did so cautiously and dumped the contents into her hand. Kernels of corn of every color under and over the rainbow poured out.

She was disappointed. Didn't an angel know she had no garden? "What am I supposed to do with these? Plant them in my window box? I can barely get the parsley to grow. Hardly any sun gets through these dirty windows."

"I have the place. Look, right across the street, see—the median."

"What, that garbage dump?" Ruth replied in disgust. "Look at all that junk—soda cans, whiskey bottles, candy wrappers, odd shoes, even bags of real garbage. I don't even know what's under all that stuff."

"Trust me, it's good soil. All we have to do is clean it up, get rid of the trash—"

"What do you mean we? How much can you

carry off in your beak?"

"I'm an angel. I have ways. Don't worry, we can do it. We can start tonight when the moon comes up and not too many people are around. If anyone asks, you can tell them you're on a secret project for the city. They'll either believe you or think you're crazy. Either way, they'll leave you alone."

Within three nights, the plot was cleared and the earth breathed as free as it had before there were streets. "Now," said Herschel, "we shall need a shovel, rake, hoe and fertilizer." He gave Ruth money to buy the tools at the hardware store.

"Where'd you get this?" asked Ruth.

"We have a fund," said Herschel. "Now, as for fertilizer—we could buy it, but I think natural is better."

"I'm not cleaning up after any policeman's horse."

"I understand. But there are other places. The barber shop..."

"I'm not going into any barber shop and ask for hair."

"Ruth, please cooperate. I'm not supposed to do everything."

"I'll do the weeding and digging and planting. *You* get the fertilizer."

"Very well, fair enough."

Using a variety of physical changes—a rabbi, a fisherman, a barber shop customer with beard down to his waist—Herschel collected a bounty of fish heads, clamshells, chicken feathers, sawdust and hair clippings to nourish the soil.

All this Ruth worked into the earth. Herschel
helped by dropping the clamshells from great
heights and smashing them into bits and pieces. He
also persuaded cats from several neighborhoods
who came to dig up the fish heads to consider the
plot off-limits for hunting, promising them *whole*
fish as a reward for doing so.

Finally, the ground was ready, the sun warm, the
moon full. Ruth planted six small rows of the
rainbow corn and knelt, with Herschel on her
shoulder, to ask God's blessing on the crop.

Each day she woke eager to see what progress
had been made during the night, waiting for the
first green shoots to break through. On the day that
it happened, they celebrated, at Herschel's request,
with a pepperoni pizza with black olives and
mushrooms and a bottle of Moxie.

The corn flourished and soon Ruth had to look
up to see the tassels. She worked tirelessly, hoeing
to loosen the soil, kneeling to pull out the choking
weeds. Herschel watched her fondly, smiling,
musing to himself, "Ah, 'Ruth Amid the Alien
Corn.' "

Ruth caught the softly spoken words and
reacted sharply. "Alien corn? What do you mean
alien corn? I'm legal. I live here fair and square. Or,"
her eyes narrowed, "do you mean one of those UFO
things? Are you from heaven or another planet?"

"Not that kind of alien, Ruth. There's a
painting, a favorite of mine, called 'Ruth Amid the
Alien Corn.' You reminded me of it, that's all."

Ruth accepted his explanation without

comment, secretly pleased that she bore resemblance to a famous painting, even one with such an odd title.

The corn had grown so tall that it could not be missed, the only spot of green in a median strip of trash, but as Herschel had predicted, passersby and even policemen did not seem curious about it. They took it in stride, assuming it was a city project, some kind of plant experiment, which had nothing to do with them. Who else would plant anything in the middle of a street?

When the cornsilk on the plump ears turned dry and brown, Herschel said, "Time to reap, Ruth." He was eager to see the look on her face when she pulled back the husks. He was not disappointed. The sheer joy as she unfurled the corn reminded him of Ruth the carefree child, dancing along the shore and picking papayas and playing among the corn sheaves with her brother. She had the same look now as she piled the ears into bags and bushel baskets.

A policeman came up and said sternly, "Hey, lady, what are you doing? This is city property. No trespassing."

"This is my corn. This is *alien corn!*" Ruth said angrily. "I cleared out the trash and I planted it. It's mine and nobody's going to take it from me."

The policeman repeated, forcefully, "This is city property and you're trespassing. Get off before I arrest you!"

Herschel flew to Ruth's shoulder and whispered, "Keep calm and keep quiet. It will be all right. Help is on the way."

Ruth ignored the policeman and continued picking, wondering what kind of help would get her out of this. A crowd was gathering. Little children sat astride grownups' shoulders so they could see the woman and the policeman better. Two television vans drove up and photographers and reporters called out to her, asking her what she was doing and why and where did she get the idea to grow corn in a street median? Was she trying to make a statement about the need for recycling, the empowerment of the independent woman, individual responsibility, world hunger, the ideas of Gandhi, and to show how one person could make a difference?

"I just wanted some corn," said Ruth.

Soon the mayor arrived and joined Ruth, who wasn't sure who he was until he told her. He said how proud he was of her taking it upon herself to make the city a more beautiful and fruitful place by her dedicated concern. He promised to open the medians to any other citizens who wanted to do likewise, and already he envisioned these havens of weeds and refuse as garden plots next spring, filled with tomatoes and chili peppers and eggplants and, of course, corn.

To help the elderly and infirm, he would hire the youth of the neighborhood to help them in their gardens. He would pay them minimum wage and give them uniforms of red windbreakers and baseball hats and they could keep the money from recycled cans, for he was, after all, the mayor, son of immigrants himself, who came to office with the slogan: I Care About My People.

As a token of the city's appreciation, the mayor presented Ruth with a hot air corn popper and an airline ticket to Puerto Rico, to visit for as long as she liked, as long as she was back in spring to supervise the planting of the gardens and the young people of the R.C.M.P. (Ruth's Crop Maintenance Patrol).

Ruth thanked the mayor for the gifts and gave all but one basket of the corn to the soup kitchen to make popcorn balls for the holidays. She decided to take her trip right away, before the snow and ice came. Herschel accompanied her on the back seat of the limousine to the airport. As she waited to board the plane, he gave her practical advice about where to sit and a bag of cherry menthol cough drops in case she felt sick.

"Come with me, Herschel!" Ruth said suddenly. "Look, there's plenty of room in my bag, no one would ever know." She made a well among garlic bagels, the corn popper, her umbrella, photo albums and ears of corn.

"I'd love to, Ruth, but I have a new assignment. I'm an angel, remember? I'm off to Buffalo. There's a young, honest basketball coach there who didn't win a game last season and the alumni want him sacked. He's in big trouble and needs help fast. This should be fun." He was smiling, already into the mission. "I haven't played in years. Don't be sad now, we'll keep in touch."

"Right. And who's sad?" Ruth fiercely forbade

the tears that were blurring her eyes to fall and took her seat. She tried to imagine Herschel on a basketball court. Would he be a player, a scout, the janitor? For sure he wouldn't be a bird.

True to his word, Herschel did stay in touch. Often en route to assignments, he would fly over Ruth as she hung laundry to dry in the tropical sun. He would swoop low and pull the clothespins out of her hand, and she would laugh and shake her head, wondering what crazy Herschel was up to now.

The Angel in the Garden

THERE ONCE WAS A BOY named Charles who lived with his grandparents in a lovely old home with a walled garden. Charles was a thoughtful boy who never made loud noises, never asked "Why?" when told to do something and always cleaned his plate to please the cook.

He had no friends his own age, but he didn't seem to mind. He shelled peas with the cook and helped the gardener weed the flagstone walk and listened to their tales of when they were young.

Once a week he had a piano lesson, and every morning a tutor came and taught him everything he needed to know to become a gentleman. In the afternoon Charles went to the garden with his books. Books were his dearest friends, and there was a multitude of them in his grandparents' library.

Each day he took an armful into the garden. Here was his magic place, this island set within the stone walls hugged by climbing roses. Here white pebbled paths marked off flower beds of crimson poppies, purple sweet william, Canterbury bells and snapdragons. There were a few curved iron benches for sitting and thinking and listening.

Three stone steps led to another level, in the center of which an umbrella tree drooped its heart-shaped leaves to the ground. It was a comforting, motherly tree to Charles as he sat beneath it, sometimes reading, sometimes watching housecleaning mice, sometimes listening to the hum of bees hovering over the roses.

Sometimes he read aloud to any creature who would listen. He did not feel foolish or lose his voice here, as he often did when he read aloud to his grandparents in the evening. Here the words were full of music and glistened and took wing.

Sometimes he just sat and did nothing, drowsily content as if he had eaten too many muffins. He would watch the lilies in the pond directly in front of the tree and imagine fairies sleeping within their cups. Charles had never seen a fairy, but he knew they existed, especially in this magic place.

The pond lay at the base of a craggy boulder crisscrossed by vines of woodbine. On a niche in the rock, directly facing Charles, sat an angel sculpture.

He was slightly larger than Charles and sat with chubby legs crossed, chin in his hands, surveying the garden. His wings were half-spread, as if ready to fly. He was not smiling, but looked as if he might, if encouraged.

In time, the angel became the boy's best listener. Charles read him stories of knights and dragons, heroes and saints, myths and riddles. In return for the angel's attention, Charles cleared away the woodbine that ensnared him and cleaned the bird droppings from his mass of curls.

Charles was sad to see patches of green spreading like a rash over the angel's body. One day he brought a scouring pad from the kitchen and began to rub the statue's shoulder. He was excited when he saw a gleam of brass appear beneath the green.

"Please don't do that," said a voice.

Charles stopped rubbing and looked around. How strange, he thought, seeing no one. He began to rub again.

"I wish you wouldn't do that," said the voice, a little stronger. "I need the green. It's part of me."

Charles dropped the pad and scrambled off the boulder. His heart was skipping with fear.

The angel began to move, slowly stretching his arms, then dangling his legs into the water.

"Did I frighten you?" he asked the boy. "Sorry, but I just couldn't have that rubbing, you know."

Charles could not speak. He knew he wasn't asleep. He did hear the voice and see the statue move. Could this be the work of the fairies?

"I've been listening to your reading," the angel continued. "It's been a perfect delight. You have a gift, you know. Even if you hadn't tried to spruce me up, it was time we met. My name is John Blessings. And yours?"

"Pleased to meet you, John Blessings. My name is Charles."

"Charles." The angel looked thoughtful. "Would you mind if I called you Charlie? Soon enough you'll become Charles."

The boy smiled shyly. "No one's ever called me Charlie before. Charlie sounds like fun. It makes me feel light, as if I could fly—"

"Funny you should mention that," said the

angel. "I thought we might do something together along those lines. Watch this—"

The angel stood up, stretched his arms to the sky and grew ten feet. He was no longer round and chubby but strong and lean, the spread of his wings shading the garden like a broody hen. "How about our taking a trip whenever you come to the garden? Anywhere in the world. You choose the spot. For exactly one hour, not counting traveling time. What do you say?"

"You're fooling me!"

"Would an angel fool you?"

Charlie thought of all the faraway lands he had read about—what an adventure to see them in person!

"Anywhere?"

Charlie, even when excited, was a practical fellow and a worrier. Before he flew off with a complete stranger, even an angel, he wanted details. For one thing, how would they travel? They couldn't very well take a bus.

The angel answered his unspoken question. "You simply grab hold of my wings—see, I can flatten myself out, then you jump on and get a good grip—and we fly. Name the place, and we're there in a jiffy."

"Won't people think us a strange sight?"

"Only you can see me," said the angel. "You're small, you'll blend in nicely. And you're a child. Grownups tend not to notice children."

"How long will it take us?"

"As long as it takes."

"Why do we have just an hour? Suppose we're at a baseball game. Can't we wait till the end?"

"One hour, that's it," said the angel. "Here are the rules: We never separate. Blend in. One hour."

"Could we go back to olden times or into the next century?"

"I don't go back or ahead," said the angel. "I just do now. Maybe you don't want to do this after all. Are you afraid, Charlie?"

"Of course not," said Charlie. "I just want to be sure about things."

"All right, then, get on my back and we'll be off. My choice today!" The angel stretched his long sleek body, his arms straight out in front of him as if to push away the clouds.

Charlie, shaking a little, climbed on, grasped the wings and lay flat. He closed his eyes, too frightened to look, as the angel soared with a roar into the sky.

"Open your eyes, Charlie!" commanded the angel.

"I can't! I'm afraid of high places!"

"Open them right now! Nothing will happen to you. If you can't trust an angel, whom can you trust?"

Charlie opened his eyes, slowly, and gasped. Islands of cream puff clouds, so near he could touch them, dotted the deep blue sky. The air rushed through his hair and ears, and his fear dropped away. His heart was light as a cork.

"Hold tight," called the angel. "We're going to land."

Charlie hit the earth with a small jolt. His face lay in sweet-smelling grass filled with tiny white flowers.

"Edelweiss, Charlie. Aren't they lovely?"

"Where are we?" asked the boy.

"Austria," answered the angel.

The meadow was surrounded by high mountain peaks still covered with snow. They walked down to a cobblestone street in a village of clean white houses and shops huddled together. They stopped at a bakery from which warm, delicious smells escaped.

"I thought you might be hungry," said John Blessings. "Go ahead, buy something. There's money in your pocket."

Charlie's eyes grew wide and his stomach growled at the sight and smell of the pastries—dark chocolate tortes of seven layers, each filled with jelly or whipped cream or ground hazelnuts, doughnuts with custard oozing from the sides, flaky strudel sticky with apple syrup—

Charlie ate so much that John Blessings had a little trouble lifting off for the trip home. That evening as Charlie undressed for bed he found an edelweiss flower inside his sock. He put it inside a book of fairy tales, where it stayed forever.

So began the most memorable summer of his life. Every day, except when it rained, he traveled to a new land with the angel. And what a time they had! They rode camels in Arabia and dogsleds in Alaska, sailed in a gondola in Venice and a canal boat in England. They played drums on a Japanese

beach and tambourines in a gypsy band, trampled
grapes in Italy, danced with bears in a Russian
circus, flew in a hot-air balloon (John Blessings
found it boring, much too slow) and took steam
baths in Finland. It was a summer of incredible
marvels.

Charlie could not bear for it to end, but he
knew that it must, for in September he would go
away to school.

On their last afternoon (they had gone to an
island to count puffins), Charlie said tearfully, "I
will be back, John Blessings, I promise."

"I know you will," said the angel, smiling. "Keep
well and study hard, Charlie."

And so on a September day, they said good-bye.
Soon Charlie was deep into his studies, and the
angel was covered with brittle leaves and then a
blanket of snow.

At first Charlie thought of the angel all the
time, wishing he could share his new life with him.
During the lonely times, and there were many, he
would take out his memories and turn them over
slowly, one by one, like playing cards, savoring
them. Then, as months turned to years, the memory
of his trips with the angel became a faraway, sweet
old fragrance.

Charlie became such a scholar that he won
awards to study in many countries. He became a
well-known professor who lectured on knights and
dragons, heroes and saints, myths and riddles, and
everyone called him Sir Charles.

He was so busy lecturing and traveling, he did

not return to the lovely house with the walled
garden for many years. Then, one night, he
dreamed of the lily pond and John Blessings. The
dream was so real, he could even smell the
roses—and he decided he didn't want to be busy
and famous anymore. He packed up his pens and
books and went back to become the master of the
home that had waited patiently for his return.

He went directly to the garden, and although it
was overrun with thistles and burdock, the gate
broken, the wall crumbling, the magic was there, as
if he had never left. Occasionally, he saw a familiar
flower, a descendant of those of his youth,
struggling to push through the weeds.

He called out, "John Blessings! I'm back!"

But the statue was gone, the lily pond dried up.
The umbrella tree had fallen over and was covered
with moss and mushrooms. Charlie was desolate.
Had the angel been sold or broken?

He walked back through the undergrowth, back
to the toolshed, where he brushed away the
cobwebs and searched in the dark corners. He
pushed aside rakes and watering cans, and there,
sitting in a wheelbarrow, was John Blessings,
greener than ever!

"My friend!" cried Charlie. "Here you are! I was
so afraid you were gone forever."

"Charlie, you're back!" said the angel. "It's
about time. I thought you'd never come! My, aren't
you the gentleman with your vest and gold
watch—a professor, if I've heard rightly?"

"Yes, I was, but that's all done. I'm back home

to stay." Tears came into his eyes and trickled down his cheeks. "Ah, John Blessings, if you only knew how the memory of you has warmed my heart all these years. Didn't we have the best times!"

And as they laughed over old times, Charlie carried the statue back to its niche in the boulder, jostling it just a little, for his step was not quite steady.

When the angel sat in exactly the right spot, Charlie sat down on the trunk of the umbrella tree and lit his pipe.

"So, are you up for a spin?" asked John Blessings.

Charlie's eyes lit up.

"May I bring my pipe?"

"Yes, but don't drop ashes on my wings. Where shall we go?"

"You choose," said Charlie politely.

"All right, then," said John Blessings, "climb aboard! You know the rules. Don't separate. Blend in. Exactly one hour, not counting traveling time."

A Tree Full of Angels

THERE ONCE WAS a young photographer who seemed to have everything he needed for a life of reasonable contentment. He owned his own studio and home in the small town in which he was born and raised. He was cheerful, polite, smart (but not enough to set him apart), and everyone called him by his first name and said his pictures were really lifelike.

He was almost as important as the town's doctor or lawyer or minister as a necessary witness to the citizens' milestones. With his camera, he recorded weddings and baptisms, graduations, anniversaries, each year's baseball and bowling teams, and the changing of the guard of the Rotary and Rebekahs and the Knights of Columbus.

Without his lens and skills, the people of the town would have no tangible memory of how it was at one special moment in their lives. But the photographer did not value his work as they did. He considered his life as a day-by-day piling up of dull work with boring subjects, a life lived on the shallow surface of meaninglessness. He had not yet tapped into the reality of truth and beauty. For this, he would have to be not just a photographer but an artist, who made photography his life as well as his living.

And not just *any* kind of artist. He wanted to be

a naturalist/hiker/mountain climber/*photographer*
who traveled to remote forests/preserves/deserts to
seek out the unique truth and beauty of each. His
coffee table and kitchen counter and bedstand and
the shelf above the toilet were crammed with
magazines and books about photography and other
arts, and stories of adventurers who had trekked
across the Himalayas, hiked the Appalachian Trail
and the Pennine Way, scaled the highland
mountains in Scotland and the Tatras in Poland,
and who had written their tales of how and why
they had done it.

Newspaper clippings and pictures of mountains—
mountains peaked in snow, towering above oceans,
dotted with sheep or flowers—covered the walls of
his studio. Two posters hung on the wall at the foot
of his bed, where he would read the first thing each
morning:

I lift my eyes unto the hills.
Psalm 121

Life is either a daring adventure or nothing.
Helen Keller

The photographer did not consider his life an
adventure. It was, he thought, a speck of mediocre
existence, certainly nothing to write a book about.
It was dealing with squalling babies with gaping
mouths and running noses, most of them not even
attractive, although to watch their parents, you
would think there never had been such a heaven-

sent gift as their offspring.

It was trying to loosen up the members of the Business Women's League, making them say *fuzzy chicken* (instead of *cheese*) to produce agreeable smiles. It was patiently listening to the twicetold tales of the older folks and arranging their wrinkled faces and bodies, which defied gravity, into compositions of mature dignity. It was always trying to show people not as they were but as they imagined they were, or wished they were.

No, he knew his gift was not in human portraiture. His gift would be found in nature, in the immovable, implacable, inscrutable Buddha mountains, and in trees, especially winter trees, with their black lacy limbs reaching up into the silvery pink sky, like a Japanese print. And he had a plan that would eventually lead to this gift's expression.

He was young, unattached, lived in and owned his own studio, had no responsibility except to pay his bills. He would save his money, read everything he could find on travel photography, make lists of supplies and equipment needed, compare prices for tents and Coleman burners and learn to dehydrate his own fruit leather. Then he would pick a destination. That was the hardest part—where? All mountains drew him, but none in particular. He would decide when the time came.

There were no mountains around his town, but there was a woods with small soft hills that came right up to his backyard. He walked here often with an older, simpler, easy-to-carry camera. Sometimes

he took no pictures, just sat and planned. It was
here he came one brisk, golden November
afternoon, after a grueling morning of shooting a
wedding party with sixteen preschool children in it.
Drained of patience, he came for peace and the
sound of nothing but birdsong and the rustle of
dried leaves. He hoped to find a patch of puffballs,
a cache of acorns, scarlet maple leaves frozen in the
stream, something, anything, he didn't have to
cajole to take its finger out of its nose.

He sat down on a knoll and watched a traffic
jam of ants in a hysterical hurry to get the winter
hoard in. He bit into his liverwurst and swiss cheese
sandwich with deep contentment. A person could
be happy here, he thought, if he had nothing else to
do with his life.

The sun warmed his back and relaxed him even
more. Then he heard sounds behind him, a faint
murmuring of gentle voices. They were not
familiar, and he could not make out the subject of
conversation—perhaps it was the ladies' garden
club come to hunt down grapevines and bittersweet
for holiday wreaths. The photographer stuffed the
remainder of his sandwich into his mouth quickly,
irritated that others had invaded his privacy when
he was in such need of solace. Would there never be
any escape?

The sounds, a mixture of laughter, singing and
animated conversation, grew stronger, closer. He
looked left and right, fore and aft, and saw no one.
When the voices were almost upon him, he looked
up and saw seven angels gliding above him, as if in

a tableau on a parade float, heading for a large ash tree slightly to his left.

They arranged themselves among the barren limbs, draped in easy symmetry like ornaments on a Christmas tree, the brilliant colors of their gowns making the tree seem still bathed in autumn glory. All of the angels were women, some with flowing hair that spread across their wings, others with velvet ribbons holding their hair back. Some appeared older and were in charge of a younger one. Except for their garb and manner of moving, they could have been teachers and students, strolling across a college campus discussing the poetry of Yeats.

The photographer felt frozen to the knoll. He reached carefully for his camera, fearing that any move might startle them, as if they were a flock of birds. The photographer hadn't a clue as to what to expect of angels. Up to this moment, he had no interest in them or in anything he could not see or reason into existence—ghosts, visions, heaven and hell, UFO's, God. He was shaky about the nonexistence of God. God was possible, he decided, when he looked inside a foxglove bell and was floored by its beauty. Only God could have created those Matisse designs, and if God could do a flower, why not Matisse himself?

But angels? No, he didn't believe in such things. Yet, here on this bright, no-nonsense November afternoon, stood a tree ablaze with them. Why? At the moment, the artist would not argue their existence with the agnostic. He must aim the

camera and work quickly to catch the impossible
scene. His heart pounded—if only he had brought
his tripod, his hand was shaking so.

He asked the God he wasn't sure existed to keep
the angels in place long enough to get his shots.
Happily, they stayed where they were. They did not
acknowledge the photographer and continued their
discussions, some hovering, some gracefully
shrugging their shoulders and gesturing to make a
point. He worked silently, skillfully. He already saw
the picture blown up, in an ornate Victorian frame,
hanging on the walls of august galleries in traveling
exhibits. He would call it *A Tree Full of Angels* and
was already anticipating the fame it would bring
him.

Then, by unseen signal, the angels rose from the
ash tree and continued on their way, without a
wave or good-bye to the photographer. They faded
into the sky, and the tree was as it had been before,
bare and black and silent.

The photographer did not feel like moving. He
sat on the knoll, stubbornly reluctant to return to
reality, like the last person in the movie theater,
still sitting in his seat when the show is over. He
was trying to understand what had happened. He
knew what he had seen and the pictures would
prove that. If he decided to make them public.

He wasn't sure he wanted to. He'd feel like one
of those people who swear they were abducted by a
UFO and everyone would snicker behind his back
and say *Sure, you were....* The pictures, even just
one, might be his ticket out of mediocrity, his

pathway to the mountains. He wouldn't even have to hope for the MacArthur genius grant. Surely he could suffer a little snickering for that.

Strangely warm and tingly, even though the sun had gone down, the photographer stood up. He had the sensation that he was glowing, from the inside out, lit up like a firefly. If it were nighttime, he could light the way home. He stretched out his arms, checked his feet; there was no glow, nothing at all different about him. Enough was enough, and he made his way home, a lightness in heart and limbs added to the glow.

Back in his studio, he worked carefully to develop the prints, knowing the treasure he had within his hands. Something wonderful had happened this day and within moments he would have evidence of it. When he looked at the finished prints, there were no angels in the tree. Not a one. The ash tree was alight with a golden gauzy haze that reminded him of the angels' gowns. But it could just as easily have been the sun.

He sat at the kitchen table, the prints scattered before him, waiting for disappointment to wash over him. But it did not come. There was instead that lingering, simmering glow—was it a satisfaction, without any "if onlys" eating away at it? Was it a contentment with everything just as it was? He could not identify the feeling. It was new to him. It was as if an incandescent delight had entered through his eyes and filtered through to illuminate every molecule of his being.

He looked about him slowly, taking in all the

homely accessories of his life. The unmatched dishes in the tray, washed that morning and covered with the red-checked towel, waiting for supper's engagement. The cocoa mug that accompanied his armchair travels. The battered soup pot whose contents promised earthy, oniony comfort and steamed-up winter windows. The rocker that fit just right into his back. The ticking clock he enjoyed winding up. The evening paper, folded and awaiting his pleasure. The cobwebs artfully camouflaged within the lace curtains.

He turned on the radio and an effervescence of Mozart poured out. For the first time, he thought about the poor, dear man, composing his heart out while keeping one step ahead of his bill collectors, dying so young and being left in a pauper's grave. Now, centuries later, here sat a stranger, lifted up and moved to tears by this music, the gift of a stranger once immersed in his own struggle to transcend drudgery.

Still full with the feeling—he decided it was an overwhelming contentment—he gathered the prints together and put them into a drawer. What did it matter that the angels had played hide-and-seek with him on the film? He suspected they had left their mark on him instead.

From that time, he looked through his lens in a different way. Each photograph became a chance to capture the truth and beauty of a particular soul. In the wide-eyed, accepting gaze of children, he found the innocence and joy of pansies. In their parents' harried patience, the nobility of sacrifice—and perseverance. In the mellow disguise of age, he saw in older couples the fresh apple blossoms of young girls and the stalwart oaks of their young men.

His reading changed also. The travel books were joined by those of poetry and philosophy and matters of the soul. He added new posters and clippings to the wall, inspirations gleaned from the wise and kindred spirits in these books, until the wall looked like a military map dotted with strategy pins:

The secret of happiness is not in doing what one likes—but in liking what one has to do.
                              Sir James Barrie

The most beautiful experience we can have is the mysterious...it is the source of all true art.
                              Einstein

A mouse is miracle enough.
                    Walt Whitman

Without going out of your door,
You can know the world.
Without peeping through your window,
You can see the Way of Heaven.
The farther you go,
The less you know...
                    Lao Tzu

The photographer never lost his love for mountains, although the urge to climb them had

eased. When the Nature Conservancy invited him
to photograph their attempt to scale a small-sized
mountain in the northern part of the state, he
accepted with joy. He experienced the exhilaration
he had anticipated, along with a dizziness brought
on by the rarefied air, frostbitten toes and a
gastrointestinal disturbance.

To his passion for mountains, he now added
vegetables and fruits, finding a hidden beauty in
their everyday simplicity. He saw stars in an apple's
navel, a dangle of shamrocks in green pepper slices,
ringed trunks of oaks in celery stalk stumps and, in
the core of a halved red cabbage, the Tree of Life,
raising its milky white limbs to heaven.

> *It is better to be an honest-to-God cabbage than a
> plastic orchid.*
>
> Dom Hubert Van Zeller

The Chamber of Commerce was so impressed with
his interpretations of kitchen edibles, they made a
calendar of them and called it *Designs by Accident*.
They awarded the photographer $200 in cash and a
certificate for $50 worth of groceries at the local
I.G.A. store.

Eventually, he did print and frame one of the
pictures of the ash tree, calling it A *Tree Full of
Angels*. He hung it over the fireplace mantel. It
won no awards and was never entered in
competitions or exhibits. His clients and friends
admired it politely, although they did not
understand the title, for there were obviously no

angels in it. Some people claimed to see the angels, finding them in knotholes and clouds and birds' nests, as if they had been deliberately hidden like rabbits or teacups in a children's puzzle book.

The photographer just smiled. He did not explain or discuss the picture, nor did he dissuade those who claimed to see the angels. He, better than anyone, knew that angels come and go, show themselves or not, as they please, for their own mysterious purpose.

The Angels' Gifts

IN HEAVEN, AS ON EARTH, Christmas Eve was the apex of exhilaration. No other feast could match this night of such poignant anticipation; one could hardly breathe for the sweet, yearning pain of it. It was the time of miracles and merry mischief. It was the time when the angels gave their gifts.

And in heaven, as on earth, these last moments before the feast were jammed with preparation. Not baking or cleaning or hustling about buying presents or other human ways of showing love—the angels did things differently. On Christmas Eve, each was allowed to give a gift to a specially chosen human. The deed itself would be offered at the party for the Child. There were no house rules, no restrictions. "The sky's the limit," God had said.

No gifts were ever alike, since the angels were as unique in appearance and temperament as humans. Not all gave praise by singing; some couldn't even carry a tune. But each had his or her own work, freely chosen, drawn by inner compass, and each was happy in that work, so that envy and dissatisfaction and jealousy did not exist. They were, after all, citizens of heaven.

Some chose guardian work, lifetime jobs as uneventful or exciting as the humans in their charge. Those guarding explorers, police officers, adolescents, circus acrobats and school bus drivers often suffered from overwork. Then the Substitutes were called in, the angels who enjoyed short-term work and the challenge of diversity.

Other angels worked in the Nursery and Nursing Home Units, the Firefighters Brigade, the Warning Messengers, the Welcomers who greeted newcomers and the Special Mission Unit, which gave instant intervention in the crises of the day—earthquakes, revolutions, the Russian parliament, Italian soccer games, a coal mine in Kentucky—wherever the urgency might be, they were there. The angels in this unit loved the challenge of the question mark, the unfinished story waiting for them to finish it.

To this high-spirited group belonged Valerian, Bergamot and Cosima. Valerian, a glorious bronze radiance in orange and saffron robes, ebony mane streaming free past his shoulders, was an intellectual, a master of puns and crossword puzzles, the best of the peacemakers. He spent much time at the United Nations, but he also called on philosophers and on preachers needing help with their Sunday sermons.

Bergamot resembled a Nordic God one hundred times over. He wore a robe blue as the sky, and his long blonde hair was tied with a green velvet ribbon. His passion was nature and animals and all small helpless creatures, including the humans, who always seemed to be making a mess of things.

Cosima, smaller than the other two, was irrepressibly effervescent. With her white gown dotted with rosebuds and her mop of red curls, she could easily pass for a human just as she was—and she often did. Her favorite form, however, was a bubble. She eased the lot of the lonely and timid and misunderstood who badly needed heavenly succor. She also enjoyed matchmaking.

On this night, the three angels, who had been friends for eons, were working out the details of their Christmas gifts. During the year, as they whizzed across the country, they saw things that they tucked into memory. Tonight they pulled them out to decide which person or circumstance they would change for the better. The choice was difficult, even for angels, because there were so many of the dear little humans in aching need. Once they had decided on the recipients, they discussed the manner of gift to be given.

"It must be something outrageous," said Bergamot, "something marvelous that could not happen without our doing it." Bergamot was at heart a swashbuckling sort, who, when work was done, would sit in theater balconies and watch old Errol Flynn movies.

"And it must be ironic," said Valerian, "a delicious ironic paradox, a situation only heavenly wit could dream up."

"And, of course, extravagant," said the soft-hearted Cosima. "Utterly, romantically extravagant, icing on the cake, ambrosia of the gods...."

Valerian demurred about extravagance. "There are too many hungry, homeless, hopeless people—

what do they need of icing when they have no bread? What do they need of perfume when they have no clothes?"

"That's just the point," interrupted Cosima, who had a temper to match her red hair. "Man does not live by bread alone. He needs cheesecake now and then. A velvet cap, a crystal goblet, a rose in the snow—I ask you, did the Wise Men bring diapers?"

The angels pondered and agreed. Very well, then, the gifts would be outrageous, ironic and extravagant, for only such things would befit the circumstances of Christmas.

And now, all was ready. Every angel not in the choir was poised for takeoff. The three angels embraced their guardian friends who would be riding the New York subway tonight. They wore red berets and sweatshirts with *Guardian Angels* printed on them. "Nice touch," admired Valerian. Then they flew off into the sky like so many exploding stars.

Their first journey was to a small town in South Dakota, where the snow was already falling heavily. Houses, which looked as if they had been randomly tossed across the landscape, made minute indentations in the drifts. The angels hovered over a small, low building, dark and bleak as the prairie itself. No cheery lights shone from the windows— no welcoming smoke curled up from the chimney. From within came the muffled sounds of barking, plaintive, anxious, forlorn. An occasional *meowr*, equally querulous, mingled with the din.

"Here it is," said Bergamot. The sign above the door read *St. Leonard's Animal Shelter*. He unlocked the door easily. "Listen, they're asking us to hurry." The story the animals had to tell was sad. The building had been sold and the new owners wanted it razed by the end of the month. All animals remaining would be destroyed by December 25. "Can you imagine," he sighed, "on Christmas Day, of all days."

The angels set to work opening cages, nuzzling the kittens and puppies too young to be wary, rubbing the chewed ears of old cats and lame dogs whose eyes still lit up with hope. "Come, little friends," urged Bergamot, "your life is dear to us and those who do not know you yet. Quickly now, into the cages. Don't push, there's room for all. Old ones, keep the babies warm, the snow is chilling...."

Off the angels flew, back into the sky, bearing their cargo of cats and dogs and one ancient decrepit parrot. The bird dug his claws into Bergamot's shoulder for dear life and cried gleefully, "Holy Cannoli, hold on to your britches."

Within the hour, all the animals had been brought to homes where they would be loved— nursing homes, a prison, a school on the Indian reservation. Bergamot knew the hearts of the teachers and guards and nurses who served here, good people who knew the importance of having something to love.

Only the parrot remained, spewing his nonstop repertoire of irrelevant wisecracks. "Hey, sweetie, gimme a kiss!" "What's up, Doc?" "Set 'em up, boys,

drinks on the house!" "Yessir, that's my baby!"
"Cheer up, tomorrow could be worse!" Over and
over he squawked his litany. "You rowdy remnant
of faded glory," chuckled Bergamot, "I have just the
place for you," and the angels flew to an apartment
in a shabby building and left the bird on a rocker.

An old poet named Laszlo lived here. He had
once been a promising young poet, but the promise
had gone unfulfilled. Now he wrote verses for
greeting cards to pay the rent. (*To Teacher On Her
Retirement* had been his best seller.) He had had
several wives—but none at present. And he drank
more than he should. Tonight he felt he could not
bear the joy of the foolish crowds, the everpresent
gaiety he could not escape. He had decided it was
ridiculous to continue an existence in which he
mattered to absolutely no one. The thing was, how
to do it....

A rude, rasping shriek jolted him from his
concentration. "Hey, sweetie, gimme a kiss!" A
moth-eaten, molting parrot sat on the arm of his
rocker, checking him out. He looks like I feel,
thought the poet. Maybe he wants a cracker. No
cracker to be found, he gave the bird a stuffed olive.
"Cheer up, tomorrow could be worse!" the parrot
responded in thanks.

Laszlo did not question why a parrot was sitting
on his rocker. Poets and mystics accept mystery.
Tomorrow was Christmas, and he had been given
this raucous kindred spirit to love. That was all he
knew and all he needed to know. He would call him
Karamazov.

On their second journey, the angels entered the skies above a Boston suburb, the streets still sprinkled with happy last-minute shoppers. Snow had not yet come but was in the air, waiting. They stopped at a small library, now darkened. Cosima knew this place well in between missions. She often curled up in the children's nook with a romance novel. A woman was locking the door.

"There she is," cried Cosima, "right on time, as usual. Dear Agnes. Oh, this will be such fun!"

The angels followed her as Agnes walked briskly, crossing streets and sidewalks she had known since childhood. Here she had grown up, with her boisterous, loving Irish family. Here she had dreamed and laughed and teased away her youth, and grieved for her brothers killed in the war, and taken care of her parents until they, too, died. Now she lived alone.

Sometimes, on a night such as this, filled with memories, the ache took over, but even then, she never let it show. "That nice Miss Danaher," the neighbors called her—and she played the role, always pleasant and available. Tonight she stopped at the German bakery and bought a crumb coffee cake for tomorrow after Mass, a little something to make the day special. Somehow she would get through the rest of the day. She had thought of going to a restaurant, full of warmth and good smells and cheery folk, but she felt awkward about being alone. She didn't want to look like that old lady in that painting by Norman Rockwell, advertising her aloneness. No, she would stick it out; it was only one day.

When she got home, she decided she would treat herself to a nice hot bubble bath, and then have a good strong cup of Dublin tea. That would cheer her up. She turned on the bathtub faucet and then leaped back in shock as a geyser of water shot up to the ceiling. The faucet knob fell into the tub with a clunk. Agnes, who was not a screamer, screamed. "Help me, Lord, what should I do?" She jammed a towel over the fountain—but the churning force pushed its way through. The mirror steamed up, and the prayer to Saint Raphael taped to it began to curl away.

She ran to the phone book and with shaking hands opened the yellow pages to "Plumbers." Strangely, one name had been underlined; she wondered why, but dialed Matthew O'Toole, Plumbing & Heating 24-hour Service nonetheless. Mr. O'Toole assured her he would be right over. The angels, settled comfortably on the old sofa, smiled. It had begun.

Matthew O'Toole had the faucet repaired in less than half an hour. He helped Agnes mop up the bathroom, and when the mirror was dry, he retaped the prayer onto it. Agnes was embarrassed that he had seen it. "My mother gave it to me," she said, cheeks reddening, "when I was younger." When I still had hope, she thought.

"It's lovely, isn't it," he said, "quite different from most prayers of that era. Listen, note the Victorian phrasing...." And he read aloud, "Raphael, angel of happy meetings, lead us by the hand to those who wait for us. Let us not be strangers in the province of joy, all ignorant of the concerns of our country." Then the plumber added, "How beautifully put. It could have been written by Hopkins or Thompson or one of the Meynells."

The English Catholic Poets had been her major at college. Agnes' heart fluttered like a bird beating its wings. She put her hand to her throat, as if to still it, and she wished fervently she might somehow pull the pins from her bun to free her chestnut hair, her best asset.

She invited Matthew O'Toole to share a cup of tea and her Christmas coffee cake, which he gladly accepted—and over this sharing, they exchanged the facts of their lives. He had been in the seminary when World War II broke out, served in the Army in France, came back, married, taught in college, lost his wife, went to pieces for a while and began a new life as a plumber, which gave him much satisfaction. "Sometimes I feel like a doctor, always on call," he said.

When the teapot was empty and most of the cake gone, he packed up his tools and put on a red wool cap over his short grey hair. He refused to take any payment from Agnes, saying he couldn't on Christmas Eve. He hesitated before leaving. "I'm going to Midnight Mass. Would you care to join me? Unless you have other plans...."

Agnes Danaher replied "Yes." Simply, quietly, unhesitatingly. Raphael had done his part. The rest was up to her. "I'd love to. I haven't been since my parents died—I've missed it."

They stepped out into the bright, brittle night. Matthew O'Toole breathed deeply. "Look at those stars! Can't you just imagine this sky filled with angels? 'The world is charged with the grandeur of God,' " he began, as the first snow glinted on Agnes Danaher's hair.

On their last journey, the angels flew south to a city in Georgia, to the home of Henry Wintringham, who had just returned from his job as Santa Claus in the mall. Henry, a retired railroad conductor and recent widower, was an unhappy man. In the heart of his pain over Margaret's death, there was anger that she had left him. How could she do this to him? She had filled the nooks and crannies of his house and life; where could he turn and not see her, hear her humming, smell her fragrance? She had left him, and now there was no point in anything.

He had taken the Santa job because his doctor had told him to get off his duff and do something. His blood pressure was up and he was too fat. Get a job, the doctor said, something part-time. So Henry answered the ad and got the job. After all, he looked the part. Tonight had been his last night, and he dreaded going home. He hadn't put up a tree, first time ever. And there would be no smell of buttery cookies and roast beef awaiting him in the kitchen. There would be nothing. "Margaret, this is some Christmas. Why did you go?" Angrily, he started to open a can of vegetable soup, when there was an urgent knocking on his door.

"Oh no," he muttered, "not those darned

carolers." Maybe if he said Bah! Humbug!, they'd go away.

He opened the door and stared. Three young black men, very tall, very strong, stood before him dressed as Wise Men. Despite their regal robes, their bearing was self-conscious and they smiled nervously. Henry continued staring at them, speechless. They stared back, equally dumb at finding Santa Claus at the door.

"Yes?" he finally barked.

"Sorry to bother you, sir. We, uh, need a charge. Our van's gone dead and we wonder if you've got jumper cables we could borrow. We'll bring them right back."

Yeah, right, thought Henry, that'll be the last I see of them. He peered past them to where a white van sat beneath a streetlight.

"You kids part of a rock group? Going to a party or something?" he asked, deciding whether to help them or not.

"We're on our way to church. We're part of the Nativity pageant. If we don't get there pretty soon, they'll have to start without us. We'd appreciate your help, sir."

They seemed polite enough. "Yeah, OK. You go on down to the van and I'll get my stuff," said Henry closing the door. He found the cables where Margaret always kept them, on the shelf above the cellar door.

It didn't take long to get the van purring again. He felt good over the small triumph and for the kids who were elated. "Thanks so much, mister," said

the youngest, "you don't know how much this
means. It would've ruined it for the kids since we're
giving out the gifts."

"What," laughed Henry, "no Santa?" "We had
one," said the boy, "but he fell off the ladder
trimming his tree and broke his leg. So we're it.
Thanks again for your help."

Then the second Wise Man spoke up. "Mister,
would you like to come with us? Would you be
Santa? You're already dressed and all, and there's a
party after.... Please come, it would be so great!"

Henry looked at the boy. "But I'm white."

The boy answered. "We know. The kids don't
care. You're still Santa."

Henry shrugged and agreed. What better had he
to do? He climbed into the van, which had
Dewy-Fresh Diapers and pink-petalled daisies
painted on its sides. "We have a few stops to make
to finish up work," said the third Wise Man. "I hope
you don't mind."

And so, on their way to the Abyssinian Free
Methodist Church, they brought comfort and
delight to innumerable families who would never
forget the night that Santa and the Wise Men
delivered the diapers.

After the pageant, after the rousing singing and
praising, after the gifts had been presented, after he
had been fussed over and applauded and hugged,
Henry sat quietly with his plate of cookies and
tree-shaped mint ice cream. "Some Christmas, eh,
Margaret? I'll bet this was your doing. Darlin' girl, I
miss you so."

Tears too long held back welled up and spilled over his eyelids, rolled in a quiet stream through the crags and valleys of his face and disappeared into the forest of fake beard.

By the time Valerian, Bergamot and Cosima arrived home, the choir was primed to break out into the first hosanna. The angels bathed quickly under a waterfall and donned their Christmas robes of scarlet and green and wound garlands of gold and silver stars in their hair. Hand in hand they began the ascent to the court, eager to share their stories with the others.

Cosima, in the middle, began to giggle. Valerian and Bergamot held her hands tightly to keep her from turning cartwheels, which often happened when she was seized by joy.

"They did, you know," she gasped between chuckles.

"They? Who? What did they do?"

"The Wise Men. The Wise Men brought diapers after all!"

Spilling over with laughter, all three angels now began turning cartwheels, flashing, sparkling, spinning their way up into the heart of celebration.

The next day, astronomers on earth reported the sighting of three fiery comets hurtling upward, which, being human, they could not explain.

Hosanna

WHEN it was time for Jesus to come to earth, the great plan began to unfold. Time, place, star, stable, shepherds, journeying kings, trustworthy parents to care for the Child—all were in place. Only one heavenly decision remained: Who would be the Child's guardian angel? Or did he need one at all, considering who he was?

A disagreement arose among the Imperati, those angels closest to God. Those who went by letter of law without exception proclaimed that since all humans had their angels, the Child must have his, or else he would not be truly human. And his being truly human was part of the Great Plan. Those more inclined to apply the law to the individual circumstance believed that Jesus being Jesus could take care of himself and had no need of lesser powers.

Naturally, God would have the last word. Still, God encouraged the angels to speak their minds openly. God would listen politely, thank them for their wisdom and then decide. Sometimes God's decision coincided with theirs. More often it did not, for despite their brilliant intellects, they could not know the truth as God knew it.

So it was on this important matter. God listened, thanked them and announced that yes, God's Son would have an angel. Not a guardian, for

Jesus could have legions of warriors at his command if he needed them, but a companion angel, one who would lighten his heart and share his journey, which often would be a lonely one.

The angels immediately wondered among themselves who would be given this awesome responsibility. Michael, most likely. Or Raphael, perhaps? Gabriel had already done his part by notifying the mother. Mirabile? Pax? Benvenuto?

God smiled. "None of the above. I have chosen Hosanna."

God heard the gasps they did not utter and looked upon their questioning faces with the usual patience. "I realize she has a very brief résumé," God said, "and that she would not be among your top ten choices. But I know she will be good for my Son. Yes, she is occasionally...frivolous, and she sometimes loses sight of the mission. But what you call irresponsibility, I call innocent delight in earthly pleasures—flying kites, jumping rope, blowing bubbles, fireworks, fireflies.... She gets so absorbed in the beauty of my creations, she loses track of all else. I call that a compliment. And have you ever heard her laugh?"

The angels began to smile, too. They had no personal objection to Hosanna. It was just that she was so...unlikely. She worked in Small and Beautiful and Seemingly Unimportant on routine assignments with the timid and the clumsy, the taken-for-granteds and cast-asides, and she did well in this unobtrusive work. But could she handle the demands of royal companionship?

Her appearance inspired neither fear nor awe, and she was not regally, angelically beautiful. Raphael called her "a bit of a dumpling." She was small and plump, with creamy, freckled skin, and short red hair cut in bangs across her forehead. When on assignment, she often went just as she was, leaving her wings at home. Without them, she could easily pass as an ordinary human.

When the decision was made, Hosanna had to be called home from earth. It was her day off, but they knew where to find her—in a blackberry patch, eating the fruit as quickly as she picked it. If she were a human, she thought, she would think of heaven as a berry patch always in season and without thorns.

She came before God with berry juice staining her mouth and robe. What would the new assignment be? Something to do with dancing, she hoped.

"Hosanna," God said, "I want you to be my Son's angel."

Hosanna looked up at God and said, "Are you sure about this?" She really wanted to say, "Do you know what you're doing?" but that would not have been respectful.

"Quite sure, Hosanna. You'll be perfect. Now don't worry about it. I wouldn't choose you if I didn't think you could do it. Just keep his heart merry. Divert him when he's weary, comfort him when he's sad. And this time, since you have the gift of turning everything into a lark, you shall *be* a lark."

And so when Jesus took his leave of heaven and arrived in the cold wintry stable, warmed only by his mother's body and the steamy breath of the resident animals, Hosanna perched upon a splintery beam and led them in a first carol to Jesus, their brother, her pure song piercing the hearts of the parents with its sweetness and soaring out into the skies where the waiting angels took it up.

(It is known among the angels that Hosanna gave this melody, note by note, to Bach, as he sat at the cluttered kitchen table and wrote *Jesu, Joy of Man's Desiring*, which still breaks human hearts with its sweetness.)

It was Hosanna who came to Joseph in a dream and warned him of Herod's plot and urged him to flee with Mary and the Child, and it was she who led them to the house in Nazareth. Here she brought Jesus twigs and pebbles for his mud pies and taught him tunes to play on his wooden flute. In the carpenter's shop, she hovered about as Joseph and Jesus carved and planed and sanded, picking up the cedar shavings for Mary to use in pillows.

When he grew up and left his parents, Hosanna went with him, sometimes spiralling ahead of him, sometimes sitting on his shoulders. Wherever he went, the lark was sure to follow, into temples and marketplaces, wedding feasts and kitchens of friends, gravesides and hillsides. She coaxed Zaccheus, the tax collector, down from the sycamore to meet Jesus. She led Jesus to the woman at the well and to blind Bartimeus, and he healed them both.

She flew above Jesus as he entered Jerusalem in triumph and heard the roar of the crowds for their Messiah, but there was no joy in her heart, for she knew how quickly the humans would change their minds.

During the last supper with his friends, she did not sing but sat quietly in a corner of the room watching Judas. If only she might speak with him.... But it was not part of her mission or of the Great Plan.

After the dinner, she went with Jesus to the hillside and sat on an olive branch above him. With none but her to see, Jesus put his head into his hands and wept, knowing what the morning would bring. Would God not reconsider? To leave the world judged a failure by the disciples he loved, a dangerous conjurer who mesmerized crowds, a simpleton who imagined royal heritage—this was as painful for him as he knew his death would be.

Hosanna began to sing, not her usual burst of cheer that could melt the stoniest of hearts, but a song of noble purity, the notes strong and calm and clear. She sang of triumph within failure, of love and sacrifice entwined, of exultant homecoming and fulfillment. She would not stop until his tears dried and he was comforted.

(It is known among the angels that Hosanna imprinted this song, note by note, upon the soul of the tormented, cranky Beethoven, locked in his deafness, to compose the *Ode to Joy* and give humans a foretaste of resurrection.)

By the next evening, the Great Plan had been

accomplished. The holy women dressed Jesus' body with fragrant herbs and cool linen and left him in a friend's tomb, alone except for the lark who kept vigil.

On the third day, in the hour before dawn, when it was deepest dark, Hosanna, in the manner of all skylarks, began her morning song. It was an ascent of bright silvery joy that tumbled out of the tomb, past the boulder, into the garden, up into the first, fresh Easter sky, to announce that the shroud was empty!

From the limp, discarded shell, Jesus had emerged radiant and rosy and smiling. Hosanna slipped out of her tiny, feathered body and resumed her heavenly form, ushering Jesus to the door of the tomb where two protector angels were already pushing aside the boulder.

She hugged her massive brothers. "Am I glad to see you! And wait till you hear the stories...."

Jesus and Hosanna, hand in hand and escorted by the protector angels, rose above the hawthorne trees, soaring like balloons cut free from their moorings, rushing past applauding angels lined up five deep, into the waiting, welcoming arms of the Father.

After completing this ultimate assignment with flying colors, the question was, What next for Hosanna? She told God that she would do anything he asked, although she would prefer not to be sent into the world of finance, where she could cause chaos in no time flat, or with revolutionaries, whose humorless zeal she found boring.

If God didn't mind, she would really like to
return to her work in the Small and Beautiful and
Seemingly Unimportant, for this is where she
wanted to bloom and be of best use. God
understood and gave her the freedom to work as
long as she wished at the S.B.S.U., and she has
been there ever since.

Through the centuries, she has inspired the
invention of the clothespin, crayons, peanut butter,
earmuffs and other small delights. Today she works
in kindergartens and prison gardens, clown schools
and concentration camps, soup kitchens and Meals
on Wheels. She counsels storytellers and
comedians on using their gifts to heal and never
hurt. And every year, if she can fit it in, she dances
with the Rockettes in their Christmas show.

Her résumé grows by the day. She couldn't care
less—the work's the thing for her—but even
Raphael is impressed by the dumpling's
achievements. God, of course, is not surprised.